How ca

METAC
DAT

MVRDV

ITY
ATOWN

010 Publishers, Rotterdam

Acknowledgements

METACITY/DATATOWN is based on the video installation of the same title produced by MVRDV for the Stroom Center for the Visual Arts, The Hague, and exhibited from 12 December 1998 through 13 February 1999. The video installation was the second part of the project 'Metacity' that was conceived by Jan van Grunsven, Winy Maas, and Arno van der Mark in collaboration with Stroom.

METACITY/DATATOWN was conceived by Winy Maas. It was researched and produced by MVRDV: Winy Maas, Jacob van Rijs, and Nathalie de Vries with Bas van Neijenhof, Mathurin Hardel, Ximo Peris Casado, Margeritha Salmeron Espinosa, Eline Wieland, Marino Gouwens, Kok Kian Goh, Christoph Schindler, Penelope Dean, Nicole Meijer, Joost Grootens, Fokke Moerel, Eline Strijkers, Gabriela Bojalil.

It was designed by Paul Ouwerkerk
of Graphic Language, Rotterdam.
The text was written by Winy Maas
and edited by Jennifer Sigler.
The transcript of the interviews was
made by Marc Neelen and Piet Vollaard.
D'Laine Camp and Donna de Vries-
Hermansader translated the interview
from Dutch into English.
The installation photographs were
made by Hans Werlemann.

This book was realized with the financial
support of the Stimuleringsfonds voor
Architectuur, Rotterdam and DGMR,
Arnhem. It was first released at the
opening of the installation METACITY/-
DATATOWN in Gallery Aedes East,
in Berlin, on 12 March 1999.

ISBN 90 6450 371 0

Contents

Metacity

World population development

	1975	**2000**
Rural Population	3 231 898	2 538 902

Urban Population	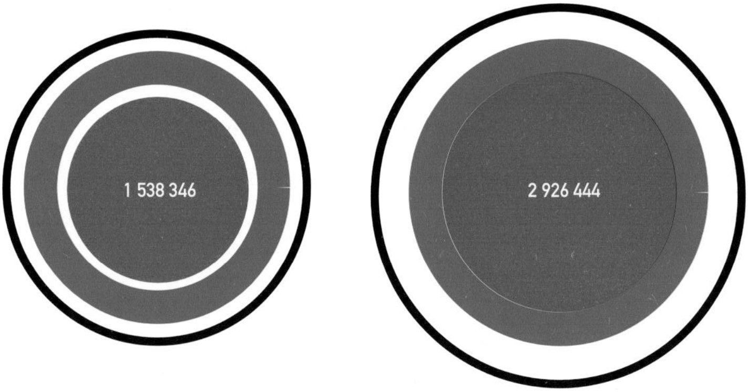 1 538 346	2 926 444
World Population	4 077 249	6 158 342

2025   **2025**

3 228 974   1 800 000

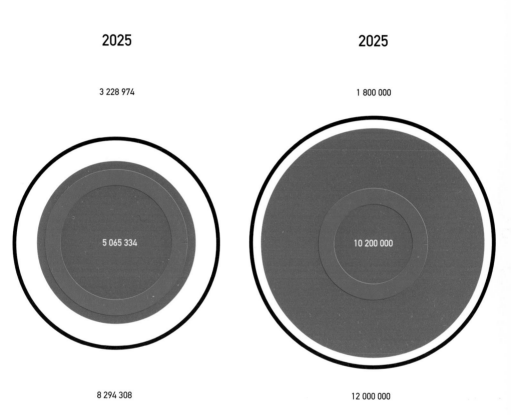

8 294 308   12 000 000

Metacity

Due to ever-expanding communications networks and the immeasurable web of inter-
relationships they generate, the world has
shed the anachronism 'global village' and is
transforming into the more advanced state of
the 'metacity'. More and more regions have
become more or less continuous urban fields:
Europe, the fringes of North America, Southeast
Asia, India, Indonesia. And as the population
and its communications options continue to
multiply, this metamorphosis seems far from
finished. Not only has this process increased
the number of these urban zones; it has also
intensified the 'in–betweens'. Even the former
anti-urban elements are colonized; they are
now concentrated parts of the urban condition:
nature has become crowded; agriculture needs
to intensify due to an increased demand and
a reduced amount of available space. Even
though this global transformation seems to
be weakened by competitive nationalism that
makes a worldwide Balkan composition

imaginable, such regionalism might also be a way to escape from this very protectionism: through specialization, each region enhances its global position. This difference, and the continued demand for the specialties of 'elsewhere', make every region dependent on a series of others, thus enforcing a symbiotic balance among them. Though other fields stress the importance of this matter, it rarely enters the realms of architecture and urbanism. These professions, in their obsession with the unique, exaggerate the individualistic. In their concentration on and embrace of the singular object, they enclose themselves within their given boundaries. Dirty realism as style-figure. Although they advocate 'discourse' with other professions and they suggest this advocacy with 'open forms', they hardly escape the formalistic.But addressing the spatial implications of this global act could actually help to define an emerging agenda for urbanism and architecture.

How to study this Metacity? Initially, one can describe its vastness and explore its contents perhaps only by numbers or data. Its web of possibilities – both economical and spatial – seems so complex that statistical techniques seem the only way to grasp its processes.
By selecting or connecting data according to hypothetical prescriptions, a world of numbers turns into diagrams. These diagrams work as emblems for operations, agendas, tasks.
A 'datatown' appears that resists the objective of style. One way to study the world of numbers is through the use of 'extremizing scenarios'. They lead to frontiers, edges, and therefore to inventions. If we imagine the most extreme state of the Metacity's enlargement of urban conditions – and thus the reduction of available space – new urban inventions might start to emerge. Looking at the world's available territories, only a scant percent of the earth's total surface currently can be imagined as usable urban space – for living, for industry,

for agriculture, for water-cleaning, and so on. Seas, oceans (which increase due to global warming), mountains, jungles, deserts, polar zones all represent reductions of the 'usable' territory for the Metacity. Does this mean that we need to colonize the Sahel, the oceans, or even the Moon to fulfill the need for air and space – to survive? Or can we intelligently enlarge the capacity of our existing domain? This observation of considerable lack of space could trigger a series of extrapolations, scenarios, 'what-ifs'... Pursuing this sequence of hypotheses leads to a town of data.

Datatown, therefore, is not a design; it is not about mix or not-mix, about compositions or relations. It can be seen as a prelude to further explorations into the future of the Metacity, explorations that could induce a necessary round of self-criticism in architecture and urbanism, and even a redefinition of practice.

World settlement envelope

Planet earth
544,852,000 km^2

Water
341,082,000 km^2

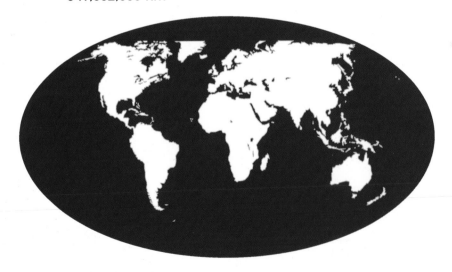

Settlement envelope 1

544,852,000 km^2

Residual settlement envelope
205,770,000 km^2

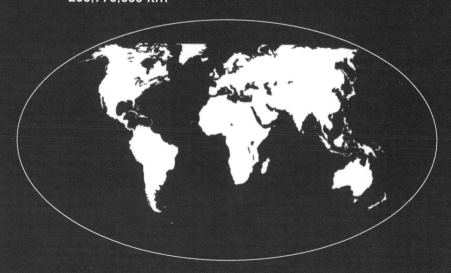

Grain boundary
45,325,643 km^2

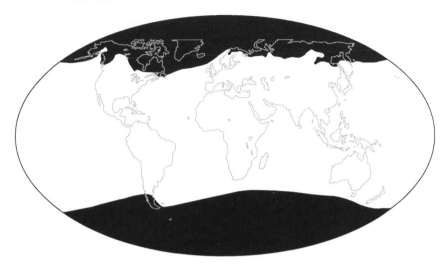

Mountainous regions
74,390,955 km^2

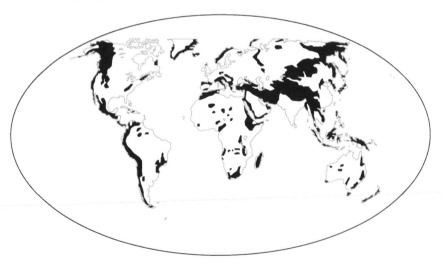

Residual settlement envelope
167,982,686 km^2

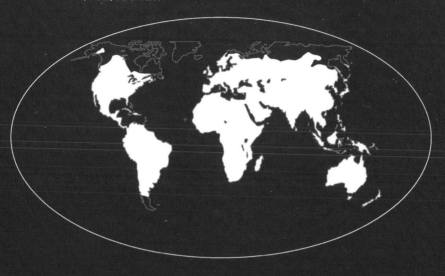

Residual settlement envelope
120,594,987 km^2

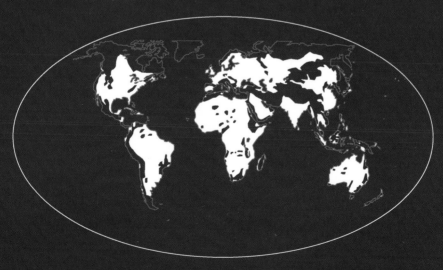

Seismic active regions
37,805,239 km^2

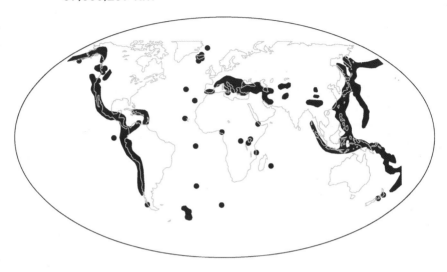

Deserts
32,452,345 km^2

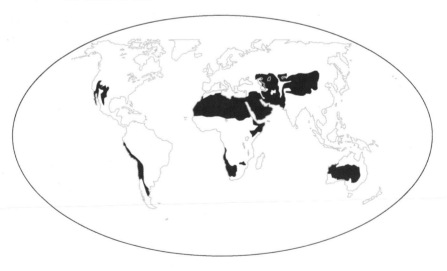

Residual settlement envelope
113,896,445 km^2

Residual settlement envelope
82,845,007 km^2

Tropical rainforests
25,631,363 km^2

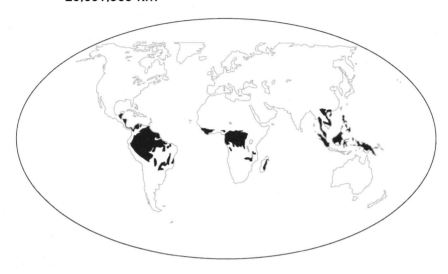

Pine forests
29,878,335 km^2

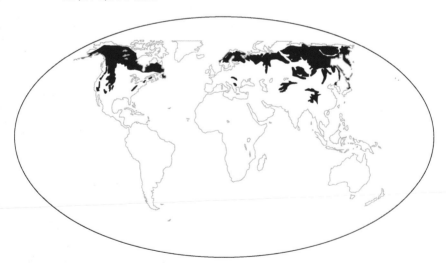

Residual settlement envelope
68,444,395 km^2

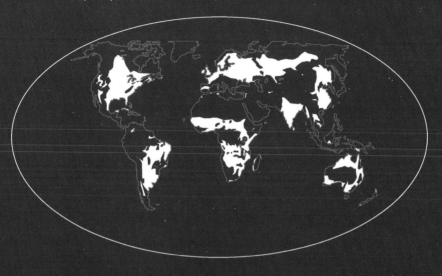

Residual settlement envelope
60,126,701 km^2

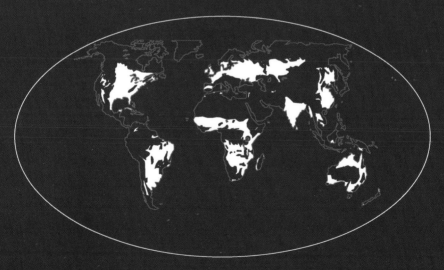

World settlement envelope
60,126,701 km^2

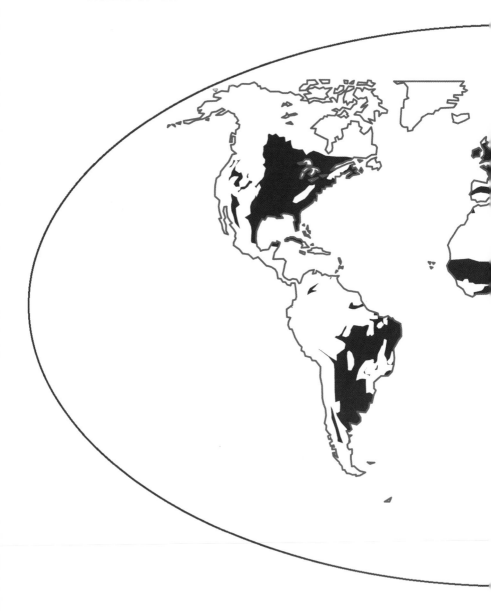

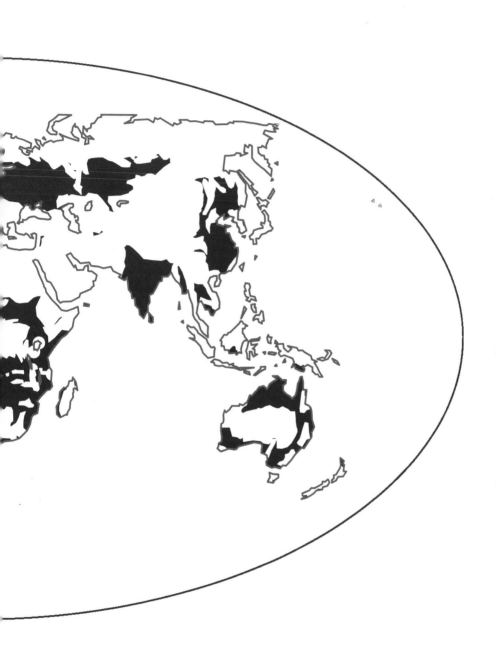

Tokyo - Yokohama
31,559,000 inh.

Mexico City
18,000,000 inh.

Los Angeles
11,456,000 inh.

Jakarta
16,828,075 inh.

Shanghai
13,452,000 inh.

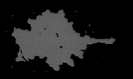

Beijing
10,872,000 inh.

Bombay
12,223,000 inh.

Calcutta
10,741,000 inh.

São Paulo
14,847,000 inh.

Randstad
6,000,000 inh.

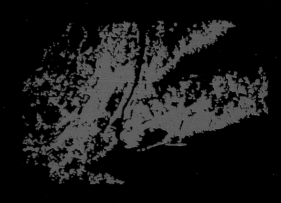

Seoul
10,558,000 inh.

New York City
16,056,000 inh.

Mexico City

Population	19 million
Population estimate 2015	18.7 million
Area	8,163 km^2
Number of households	3.1 million
Elevation	2,380 m
Density	2,328 persons per km^2
Population world ranking	3
Contribution to GNP*	24%
% of total national population	18.5%
Number of households	3,172,706

Air quality

Sulphur Dioxide	serious
Suspended particles	serious
Airborne lead	above guideline
Carbon Monoxide	serious
Nitrogen Dioxide	above guideline
Ozone	serious

Public transport, transported passengers	8.4 million per year
Length of metro and rail network	161 km
Electric energy consumption	x kWh per year

*Gross National Product

Source:
United Nations Population Division. *World Urbanization Prospects: the 1994 Revision.* New York: United Nations, 1995.

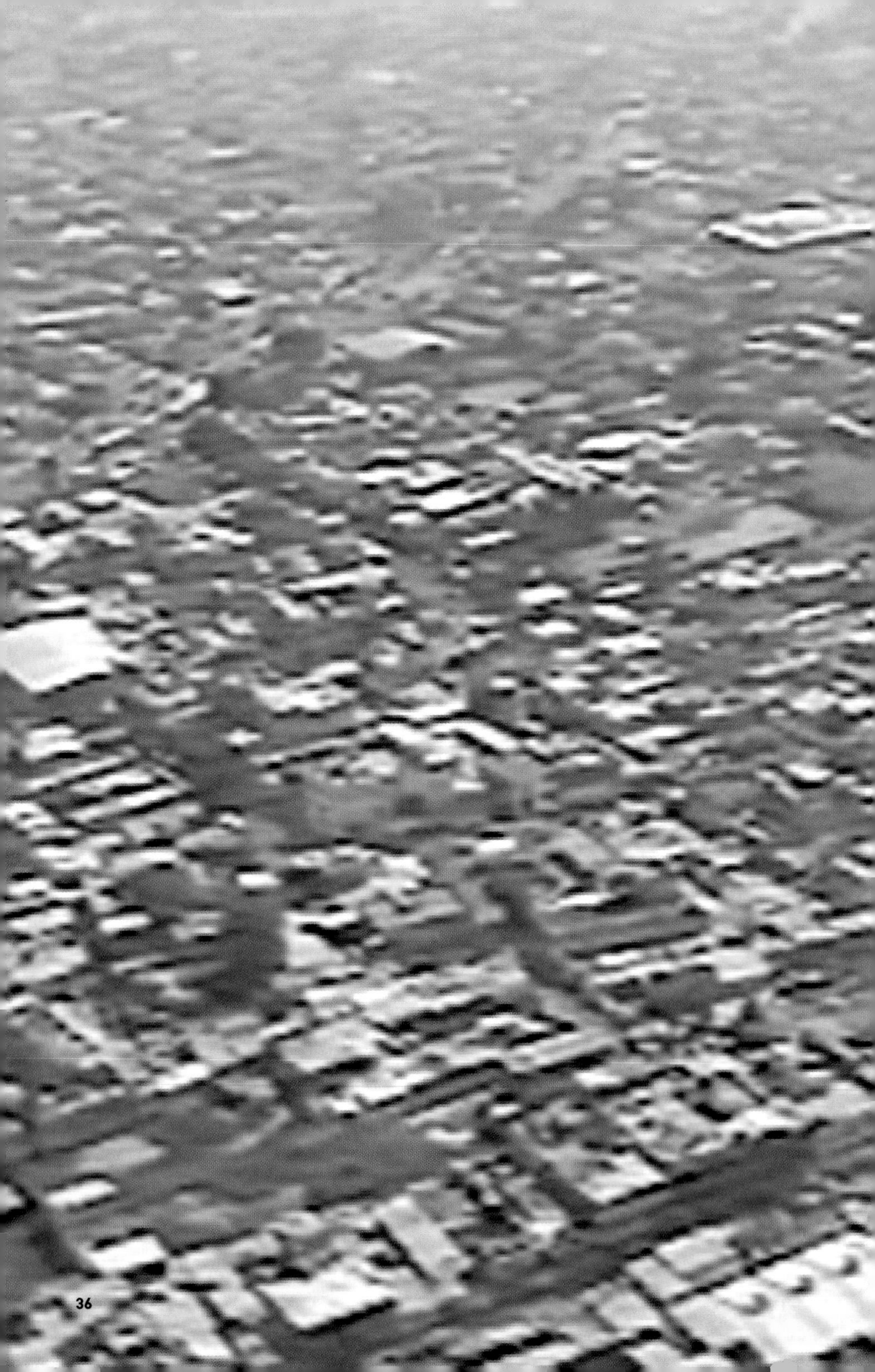

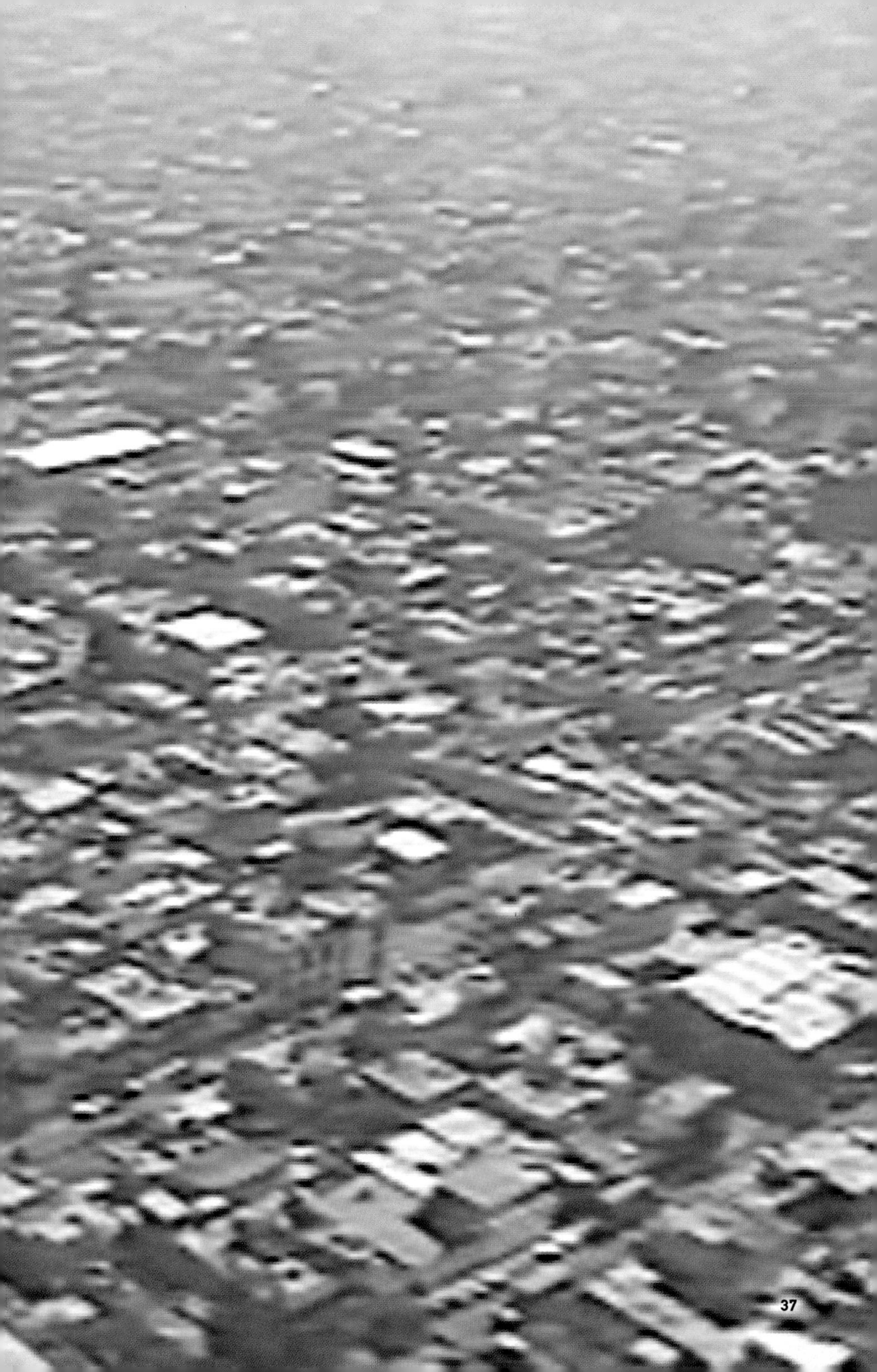

São Paulo

Population	18 million
Population estimate 2015	20.7 million
Area	1,509 km^2
Density	11,928 persons per km^2
Elevation	760 m
Number of households	x
Population world ranking	4
Contribution to GNP	30%
% of total national population	10.5%

Air quality	
Sulphur Dioxide	low
Suspended particles	above guideline
Airborne lead	low
Carbon Monoxide	low
Nitrogen Dioxide	above guideline
Ozone	serious

Public transport, transported passengers	x million per year
Length of metro and rail network	x km
Electric energy consumption	x kWh per year
Murder rate	35 per 100,000 inh.

Source:
United Nations Population Division. *World Urbanization Prospects: the 1994 Revision.* New York: United Nations, 1995.

43

Population	15.6 million
Population estimate 2010	16.5 million
Area	41,526 km^2
Density	375 persons per km^2
Elevation	-6.7 m / 321 m
Population world ranking	x
Air quality	
Sulphur Dioxide	x
Suspended particles	x
Airborne lead	x
Carbon Monoxide	x
Nitrogen Dioxide	x
Ozone	x
Number of households	7,595,000
Public transport, transported passengers	29,170 million per year
Length of metro and rail network	2,795 km
Electric energy consumption	11,253,000,000 kWh per year
Murder rate	2.3 per 100,000 inh.

Source:
CBS. Statistics Netherlands. *Statistical Yearbook 1998 of The Netherlands.* Voorberg/Heerlen, 1998.

Datatown

Inhabitants per km^2

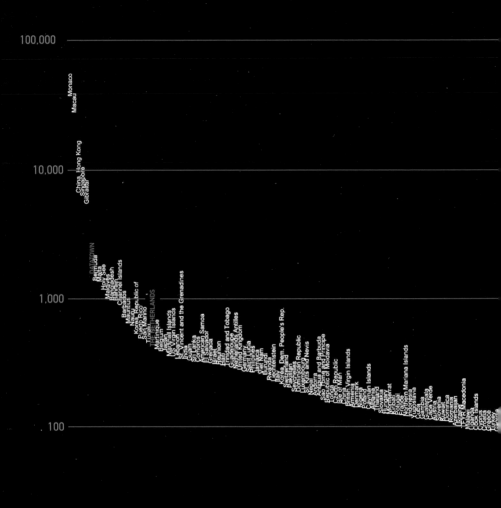

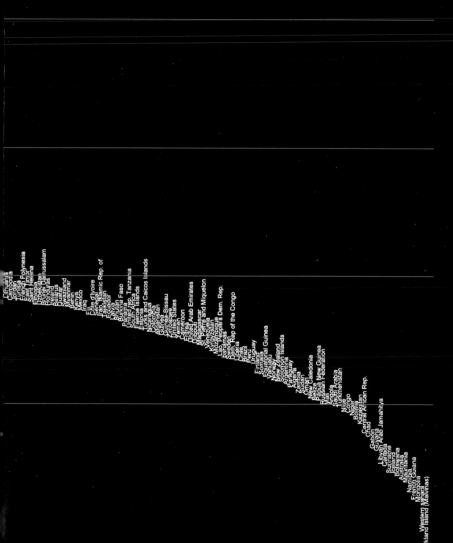

Datatown

Datatown is based only upon data. It is a city that
wants to be described by information; a city that
knows no given topography, no prescribed ideology,
no representation, no context. Only huge, pure data.
What are the implications of this city? What assumptions can be identified? What agenda would result
from this numerical approach? Datatown is based
on an extrapolation of Dutch statistics. Though the
Netherlands today seems a dreamland for econ-
mics, culture, and production, it remains suspicious
to follow its doctrine. But the accessibility of
statistical information makes it a useful instrument
for extrapolation. Datatown follows a classical
(didn't the Dutch architect Carel Weeber repeat that
recently?) approach of defining the boundaries of a
city, namely that the urban size is equivalent to one
hour of traveling. In the Middle Ages it was 4 km of
walking. In the 1920s the development of garden-city
extensions was based on a bicycle-distance of 20
km. The mass use of the car lead in the 1980s to
cities of about 80 km like the Randstad or Los
Angeles. And now, with the bullet-train, the city
can equal 400 km. Datatown can therefore be
defined as a city of 400 by 400 km: 160,000,000,000
m^2. Datatown is dense – let us say 4 times as dense
as the Netherlands, one of the densest populations
in the world.

In fact, with 1,477 inhabitants per square kilometer, Datatown is the densest place on earth. It is a city for 241 million inhabitants. It is the USA in one city. Datatown is autarkic. It does not know any foreign countries. It therefore has to be self-supporting. Its problems must be solved within its boundaries. Datatown is constructed as a collection of data. This information has been sorted and gathered in sectors, relative to the percentages of existing use in the Netherlands. Initially ordered alphabetically within a barcode field, the information was transformed for practical reasons: some zones need wider measurements in order to function properly. The barcode thus became a Mondrian-like field, compressed by its square outline into the most compact city thinkable. Datatown is based upon a series of assumptions. Each sector exists in several variations. They are constructed on a series of 'what-ifs' that embody different assumptions. Datatown is always in progress. Its evolution is literally endless; it is permanently under construction. At this moment, 6 sectors may be entered.

If the world settlement envelope has been filled up with 376 Datatowns, the world capacity will be 88,687 million inhabitants, 18 times the current population.

Datatown sectors

Sector	total area (km^2)	% of total	length (km)	width (km)
(C)O$_2$ forest	11,717.0 km^2	7.4 %	359.5 km	32.6 km
Agriculture	88,241.4 km^2	55.4 %	359.5 km	245.5 km
Airport	154.1 km^2	0.1 %	359.5 km	0.4 km
Allotment gardens	184.9 km^2	0.1 %	359.5 km	0.5 km
Cemetery	146.4 km^2	0.1 %	359.5 km	0.4 km
Construction area	446.9 km^2	0.3 %	359.5 km	1.2 km
Daytime recreation	508.6 km^2	0.3 %	359.5 km	1.4 km
Dry nature	3,329.0 km^2	2.1 %	359.5 km	9.3 km
Greenhouses	520.2 km^2	0.3 %	359.5 km	1.4 km
Industrial area	420.0 km^2	0.3 %	359.5 km	1.2 km
Living area	8,206.9 km^2	5.1 %	359.5 km	22.8 km
Metaled roads	4,180.5 km^2	2.6 %	359.5 km	11.6 km
Nocturnal recreation	701.2 km^2	0.4 %	359.5 km	2.0 km
Other	16,124.8 km^2	10.1 %	359.5 km	44.9 km
Park	620.3 km^2	0.4 %	359.5 km	1.7 km
Public transport	404.6 km^2	0.3 %	359.5 km	1.1 km
Recreational water	131.0 km^2	0.1 %	359.5 km	0.4 km
Scrapyard	238.9 km^2	0.1 %	359.5 km	0.7 km
Services	273.6 km^2	0.2 %	359.5 km	0.8 km
Sports	1,009.5 km^2	0.6 %	359.5 km	2.8 km
Surface water	18,945.2 km^2	11.9 %	359.5 km	52.7 km
Unmetaled roads	554.8 km^2	0.3 %	359.5 km	1.5 km
Waste dump	372.0 km^2	0.1 %	359.5 km	1.0 km
Water reservoir	46.2 km^2	0.0 %	40.5 km	1.1 km
Wet nature	2,211.6 km^2	1.4 %	359.5 km	6.2 km
Total	159,406.3 km^2			

Datatown plan

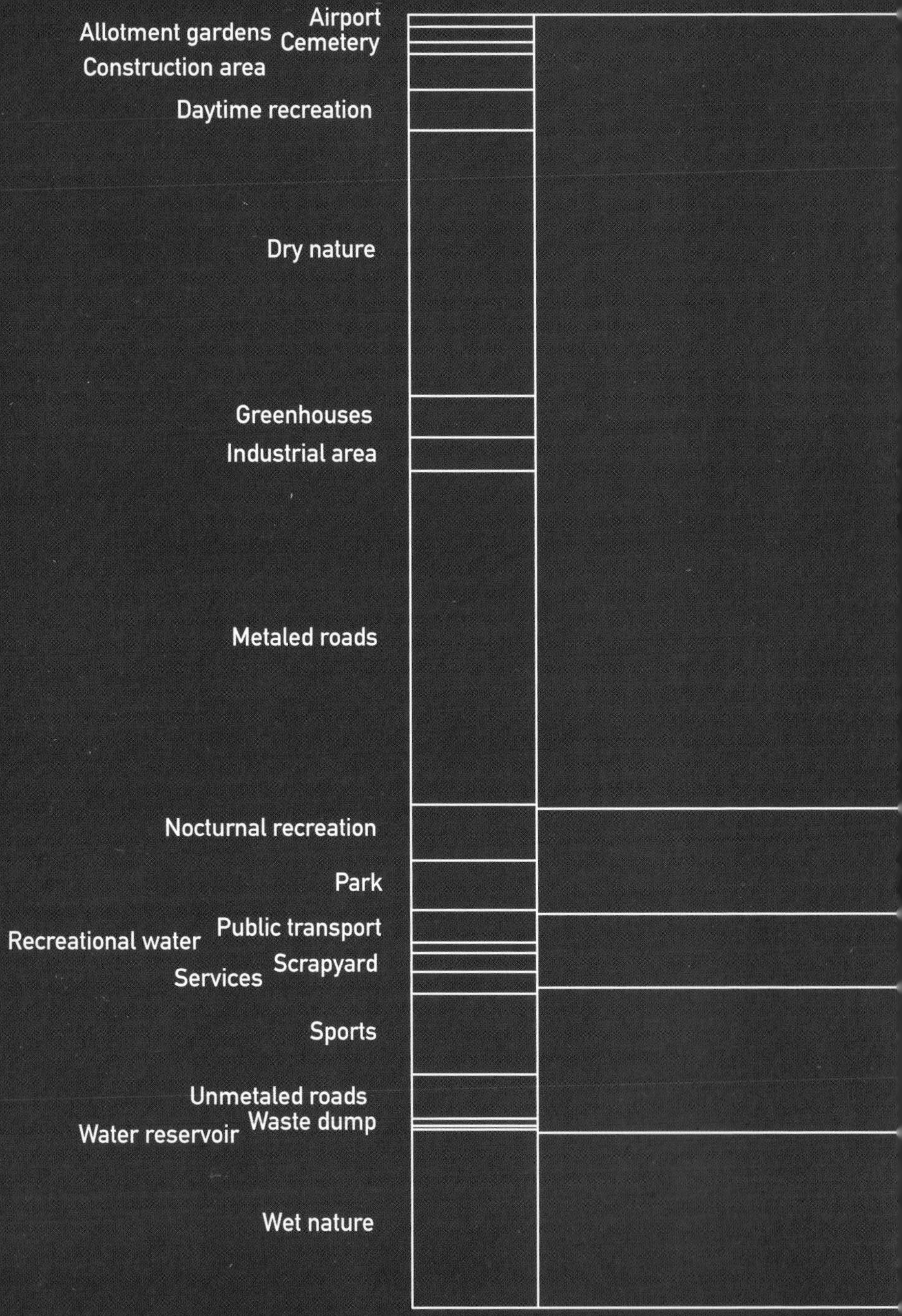

Airport
Allotment gardens Cemetery
Construction area
Daytime recreation

Dry nature

Greenhouses
Industrial area

Metaled roads

Nocturnal recreation

Park

Recreational water Public transport
Scrapyard
Services

Sports

Unmetaled roads
Water reservoir Waste dump

Wet nature

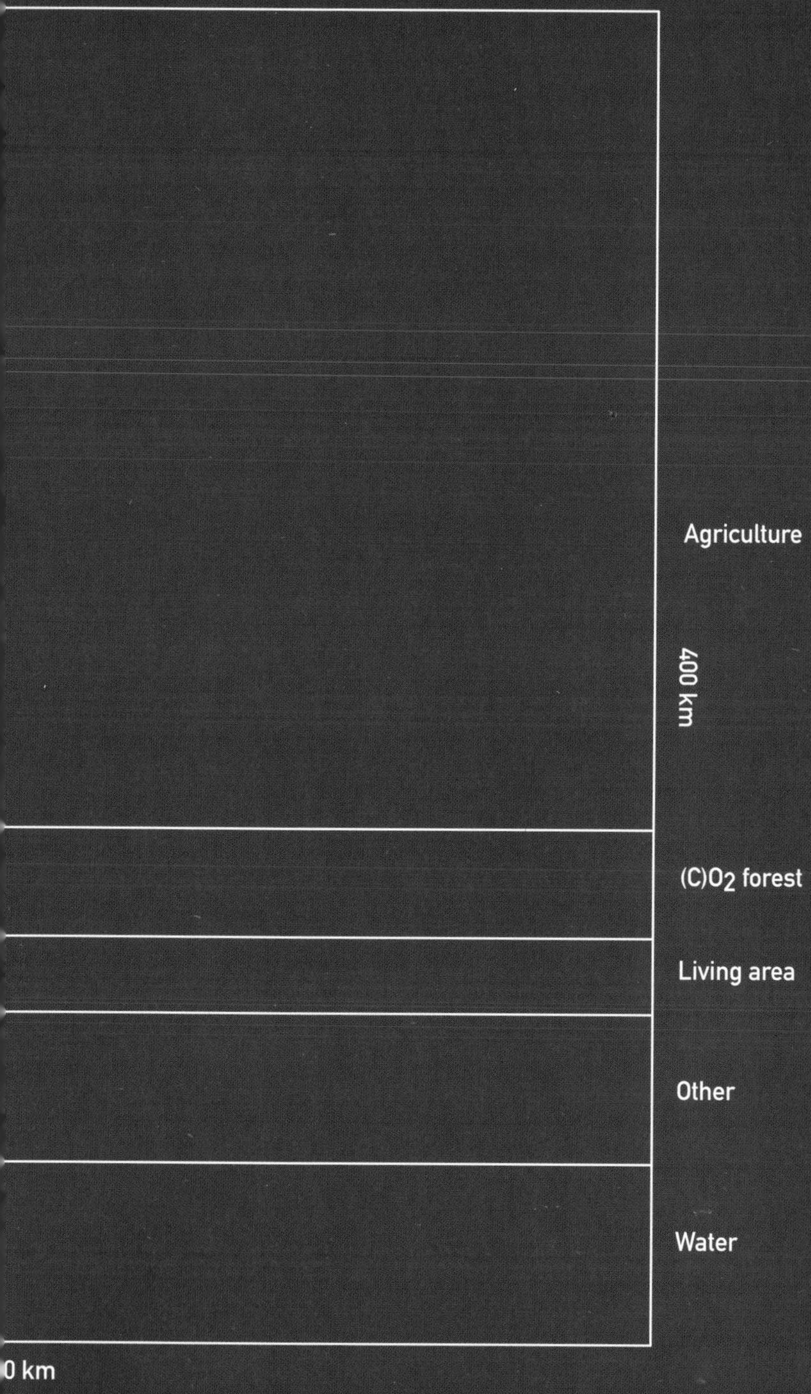

Agriculture

400 km

(C)O$_2$ forest

Living area

Other

Water

0 km

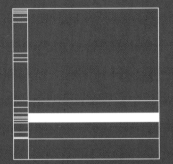

You are entering Sector Living.
The reserved area is 8,206.89 km^3

Following Dutch standards, the 241,074,556
inhabitants of Datatown live with an average
of 2.43 persons in one unit.
This yields a zone composed of 99,197,560
houses.
The average unit has 126 m^2 indoor space of
2.8 meters height and 126 m^2 outdoor space
of approximately 5.6 meters.
This equals respectively 354 m^3 and 708 m^3.
It totals to 1,064 m^3 per unit or 438 m^3 per
person.
The total volume of the living zone is
43,448,531,280 m^3.

To what perspectives does this lead?

If we all lived within one massive volume, this cube would

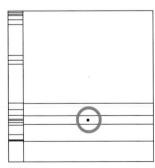

Cube
0.03% of Sector Living
Local FAR: 362

measure 3.5 km^3, with a length, width, and height of 1.52 km.

If we all lived in free–standing houses on plots of 1,400 m^2, 1,388,765.8 km^2, or 169 times the reserved area.

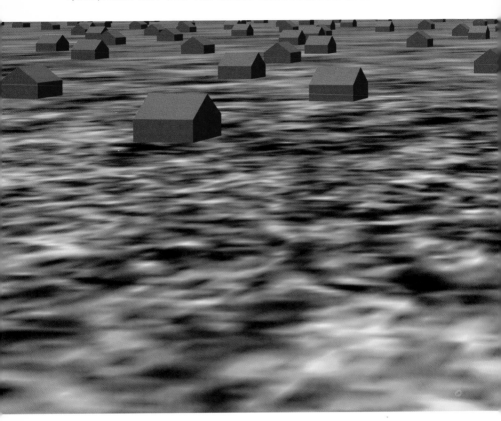

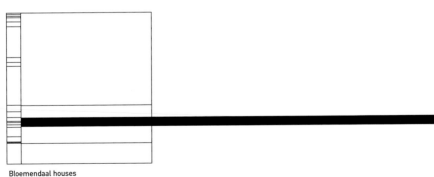

Bloemendaal houses
2800% of Sector Living
FAR: 0.04

as in Bloemendaal, The Netherlands, we would need

Free-standing houses in Bloemendaal, The Netherlands

Number of floors	1-2
Site coverage	5.0%
Average unit size	1,400 m^2
Units per km^2	714
FAR	0.04

If confined to the reserved area, 5,859,084 of these plots would be or 17% of the total population. The remaining 83% would be 1.52 x 1.52 x 1.26 km.

realized. These villas would be occupied by 14,061,801 people condensed in a massive housing block measuring

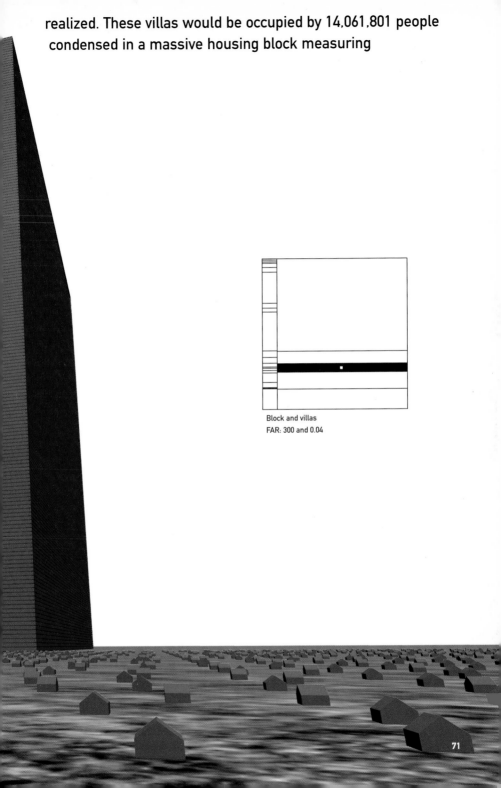

Block and villas
FAR: 300 and 0.04

If we all lived in Barcelona–blocks,

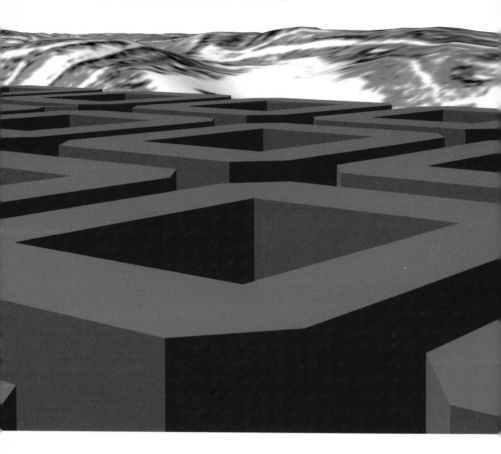

Barcelona-blocks
70% of Sector Living
FAR: 4.5

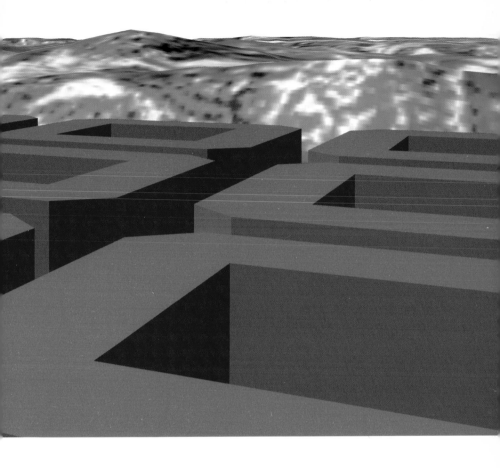

Housing blocks in Barcelona, Spain

Dimensions	104 m x 104 m
Number of floors	5-7
Site coverage	70%
Average unit size	150 m^2
Units per km^2	20,500
FAR	4.5

36% of the area reserved for housing could become parks.

That corresponds to 736 (New York) Central Parks.

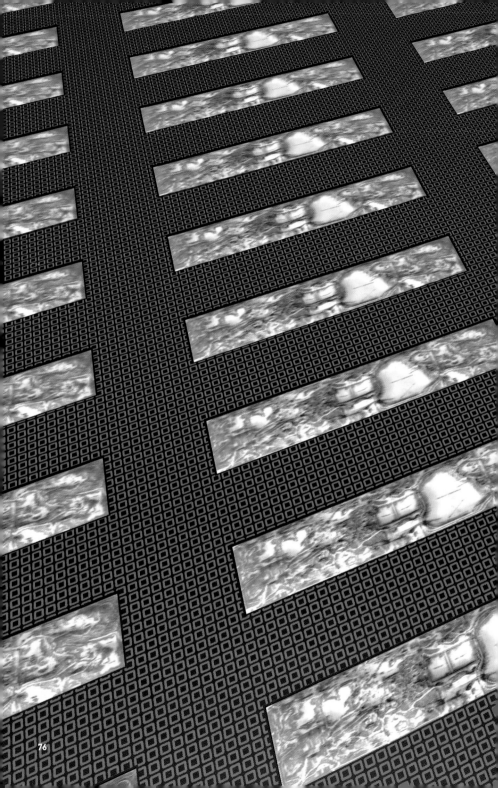

If we aligned our living space with the Hong Kong model,

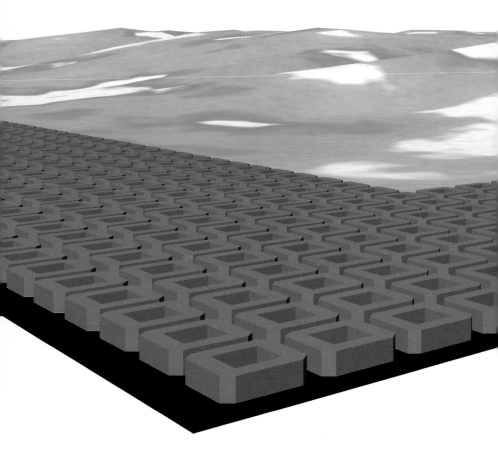

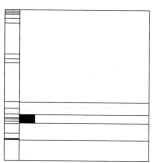

Barcelona-blocks
with Hong Kong-units
9% of Sector Living
FAR: 4.5

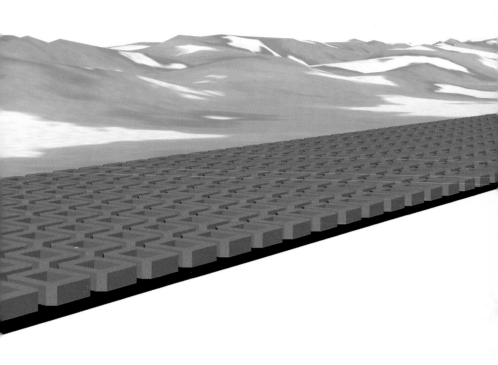

Unit sizes

Dutch average of new buildings 1998	125 m^2 per unit
Bloemendaal, The Netherlands	350 m^2 per unit
Staten Quarter, The Hague, The Netherlands	200 m^2 per unit
Barcelona Block, Plan Cerda	150 m^2 per unit
Hong Kong Tower	9 m^2 per person
Villes-Tours, Le Corbusier	10 m^2 per person

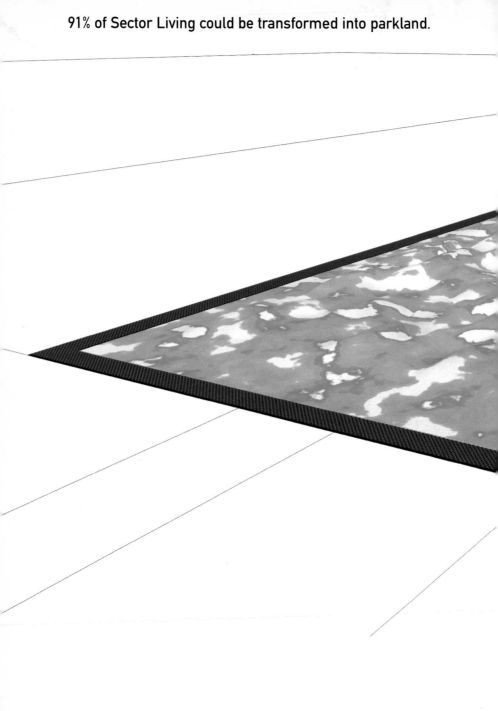

That would correspond to a gigantic park of 7,423 km^2.

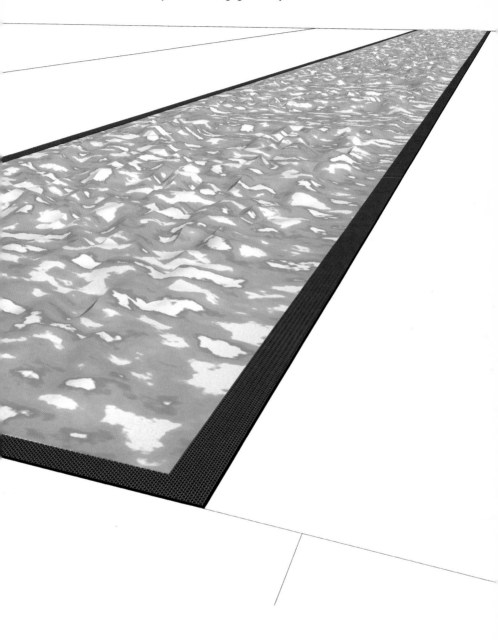

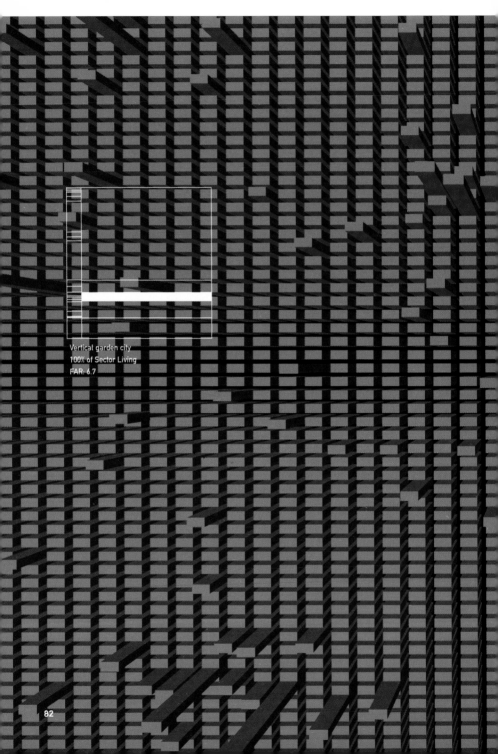

Vertical garden city
100% of Sector Living
FAR: 6.7

Sector Living.

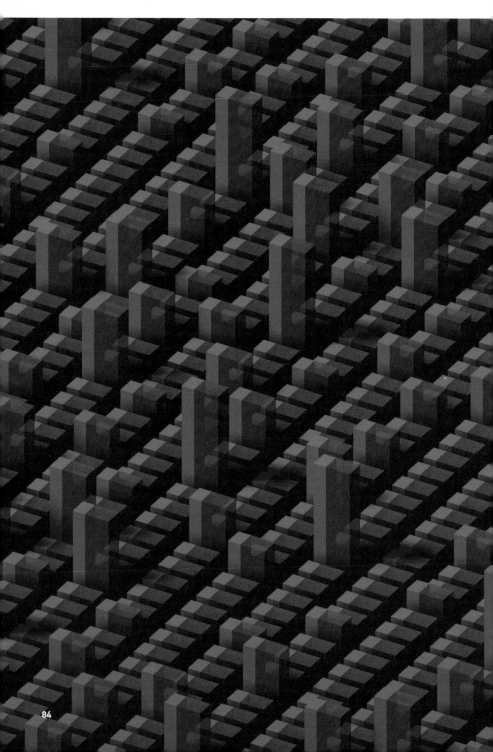

with streets of 10 and 5 meters wide,

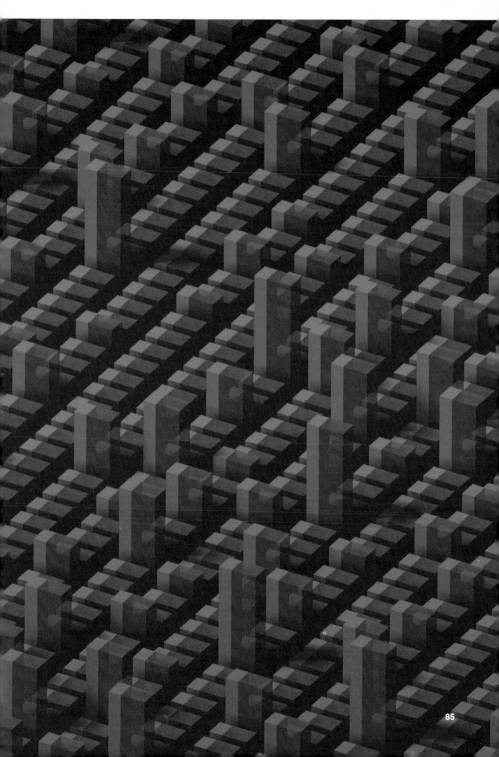

and an average height of 28 meters, or 10 stories.

The sector would turn into a vertical garden city.

Living per unit	354 m^3	33%
Garden per unit	708 m^3	66%
Living per unit	126 m^2	50%
Garden per unit	126 m^2	50%
Living floors		10
Garden floors		5
FAR		6,7

A contemporary Borobudur.

An urban density with suburban qualities: light, air, green.

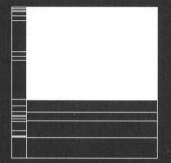

You are entering Sector Agriculture.
The reserved area is 88,241 km^2.

Since Datatown is autarkic, it has to produce its
own food. How much does the average inhabitant
consume per year? How much must we add for
pets and other animals? How can this consumption be translated into ground–use?

Sector Agriculture consists of millions of individual farming plots.

These plots are sorted into zones.

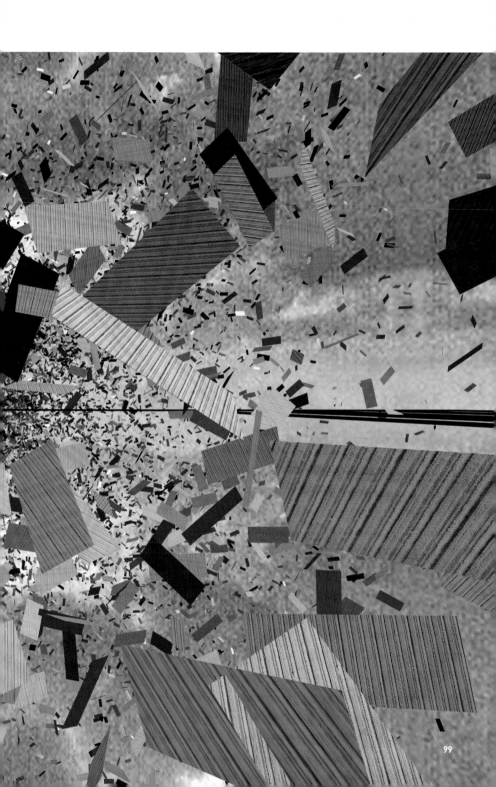

Wheat product consumption per capita = 86.25 kg = 69 kg wheat flour or meal = 112 m² per capita = 26389 km² for the total population.

Potato consumption per capita = 82 kg = 18 m² per capita = 4,376 km² for the total population.

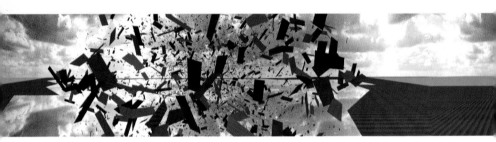

Sugar consumption per capita = 37.7 kg = 290 kg sugarbeets = 49 m² per capita = 11,663 km² for the total population.

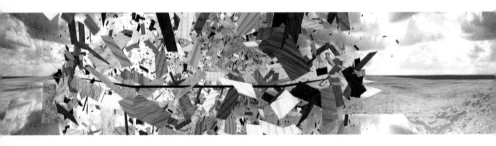

Wine consumption per capita = 17.1 liter = 34.2 kg grapes = 34.2 m² per capita = 8,068 km² for the total population.

Pork consumption per capita = 46.3 kg = 0.37 pig = 186.1 m² crops for animal fodder per capita = 44,017 km² crops for the total population.

Lamb consumption per capita = 1.3 kg = 0.02 lamb = 21.3 m² of grassland + 5.9 m² crops for animal fodder per capita = 5,026 km² grassland + 1,408 km² crops for the total population.

Poultry consumption per capita = 20.1 kg = 3.08 chickens = 39.5 m² crops for animal fodder per capita = 9,341 km² crops for the total population.

Fish consumption per capita = 23.9 kg = 20 m² of fishfarm = 47.0 m² crops for animal fodder per capita = 4,723 km² of fish farm + 11,089 km² of crops for the total population.

The total required area for agriculture is 814,215 km2.

This equals 5 times the total area of Datatown.

Meat–eating society

If we change our eating habits – become vegetarians for instance –

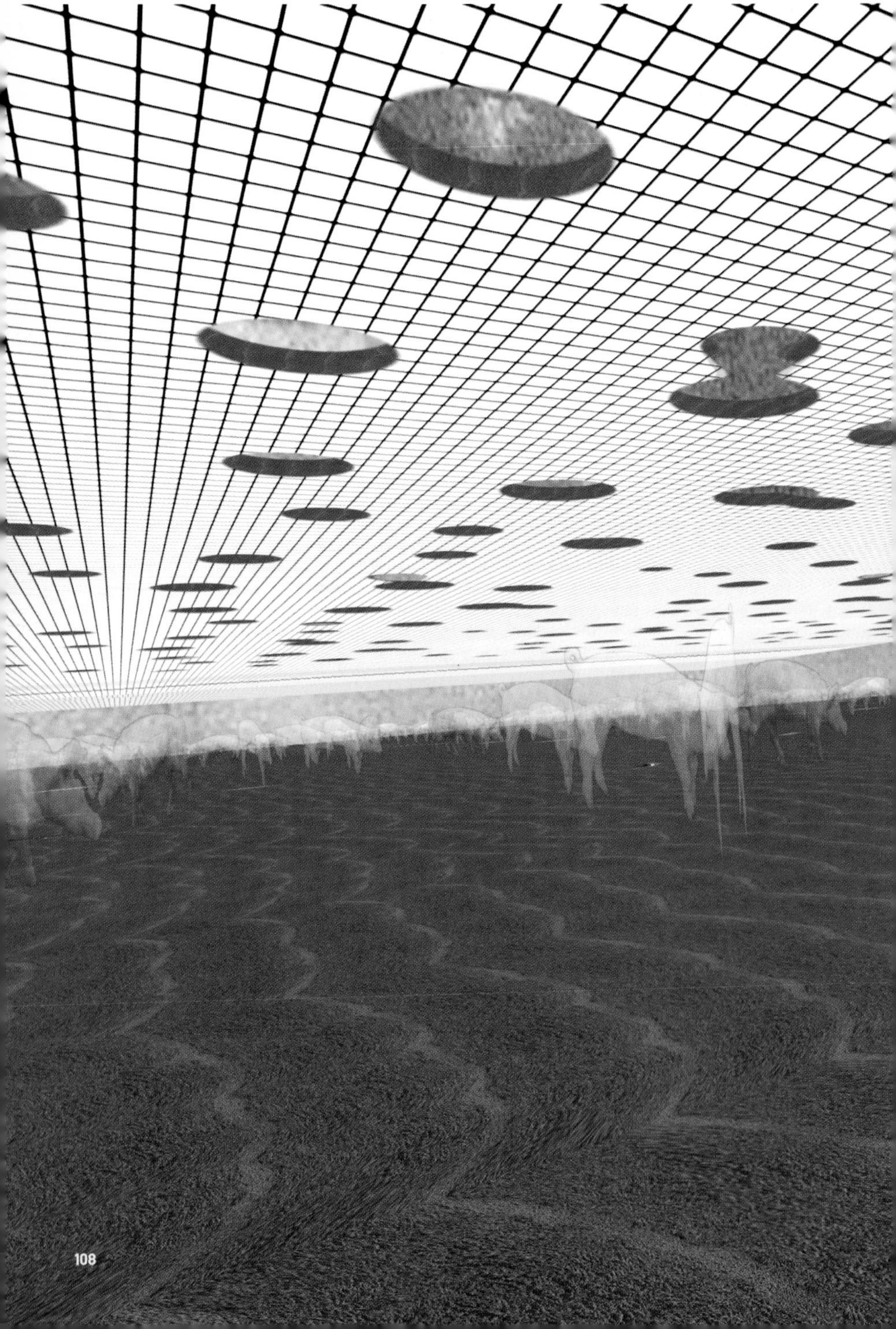

the necessary space for agriculture will also drastically change.

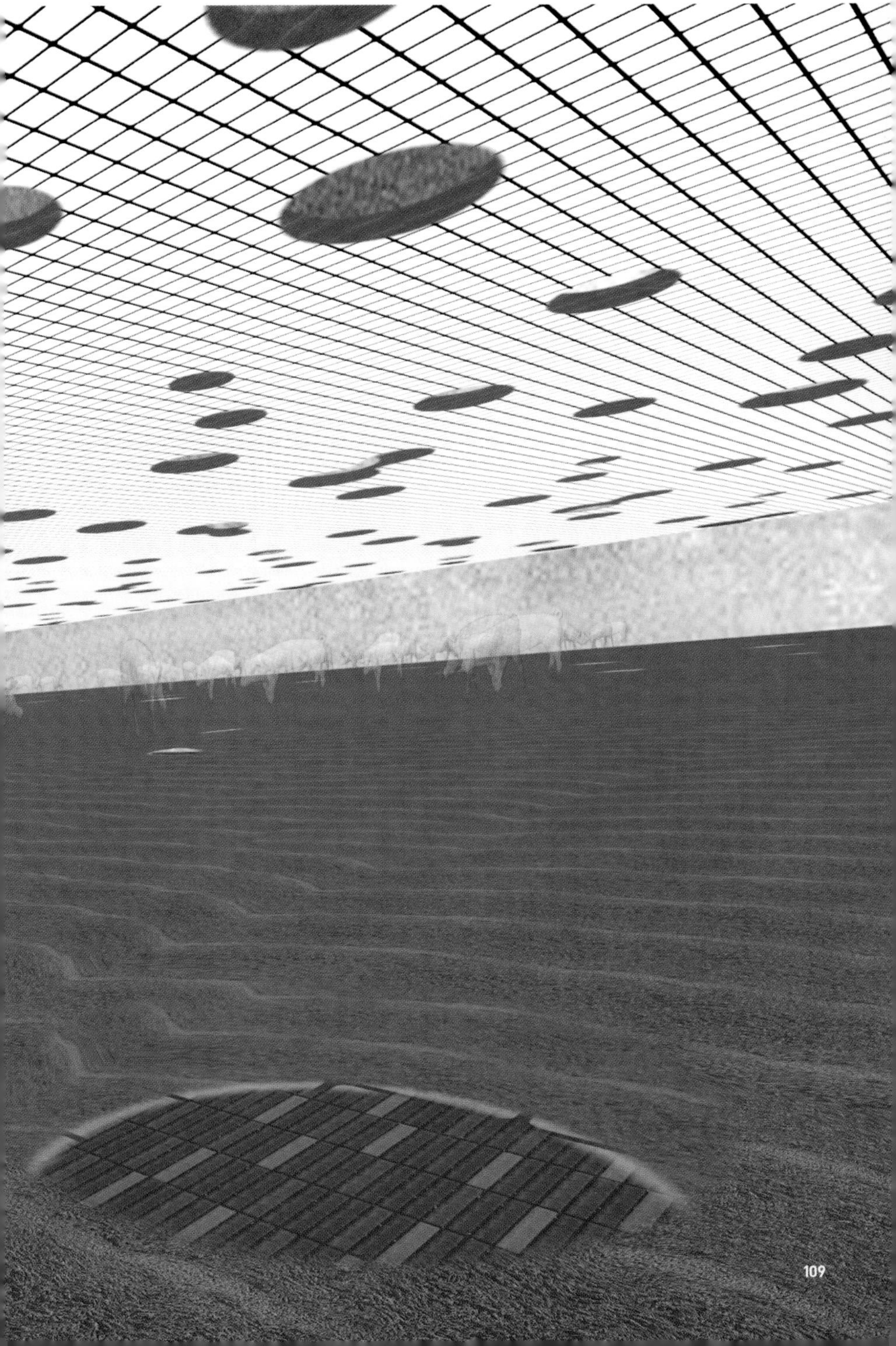

No meat: subtract 81,876 km^2 of crops for animal fodder;

subtract 56,817 km² of grassland;

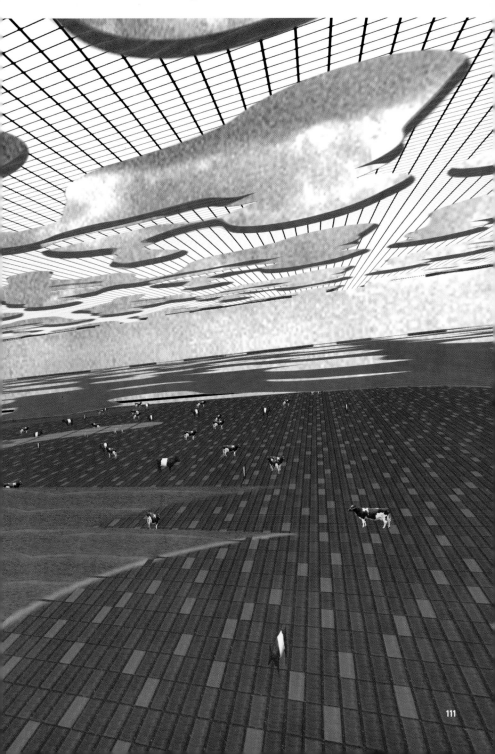

and add 5% more vegetables,

10% more milk products,

25% more eggs,

25% more fish,

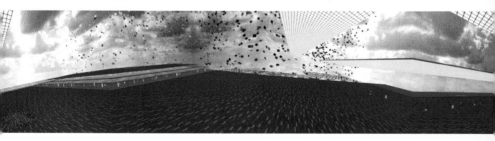

and a massive consumption of soy products.

This meatless alternative needs 459,414 km2. It equals 2.9 times needed for a meat-eating society.

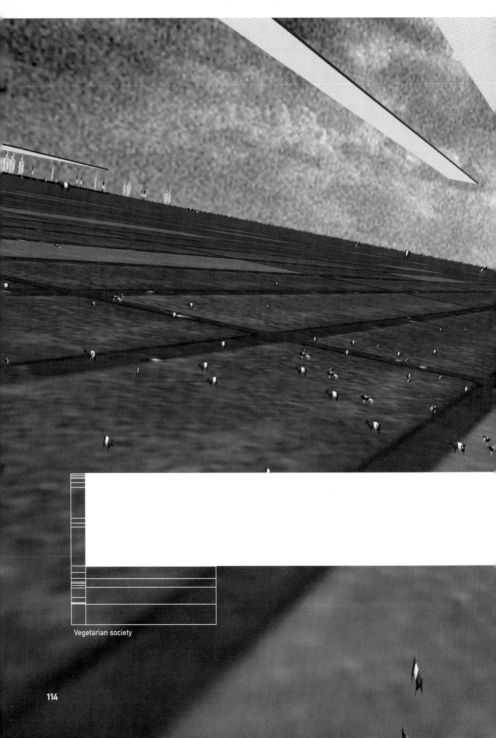

Vegetarian society

the total area of Datatown. This is almost half of the territory

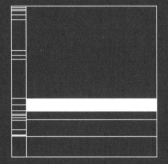

You are entering Sector (C)O$_2$, the forest of
Datatown. The reserved area equals 11,717 km^2.

Plants convert carbon dioxide into oxygen and
carbon through photosynthesis. This chemical
reaction could be used to absorb the CO_2 that is
released by the burning of fossil fuels, by cars,
by factories. Can we imagine one forest that
absorbs all CO_2 that is produced in Datatown?
How big does this forest have to be? The total CO_2
output of Datatown is 2,351,871,200 tons per year.

In a Dutch climate the poplar is the most efficient
tree for absorbing CO_2. It absorbs 800 tons per
year per adult tree.

To absorb all CO_2, 2,939,839 km^2 of poplar forest
is needed. This equals 0.7 times the Amazon,
294 times the Black Forest, or 1,212,055 times
New York's Central Park. This is an area 18 times
the total surface of Datatown, a space too large
to accommodate on a single plane.

When stacked on the given territory, this forest is 251 stories high. leads to a structure with a height of 6,275 meters.

The need for 20 meter-high 'growing-space' and 5 meter-deep soil,

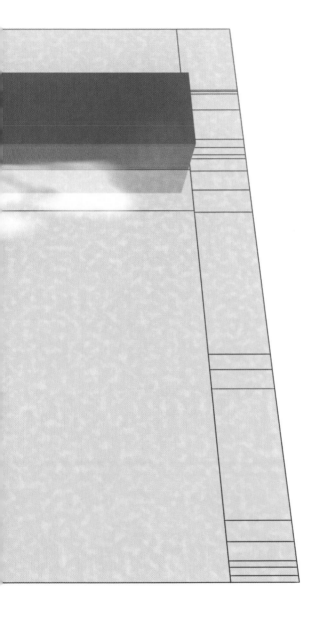

The forest becomes a CO_2 machine.

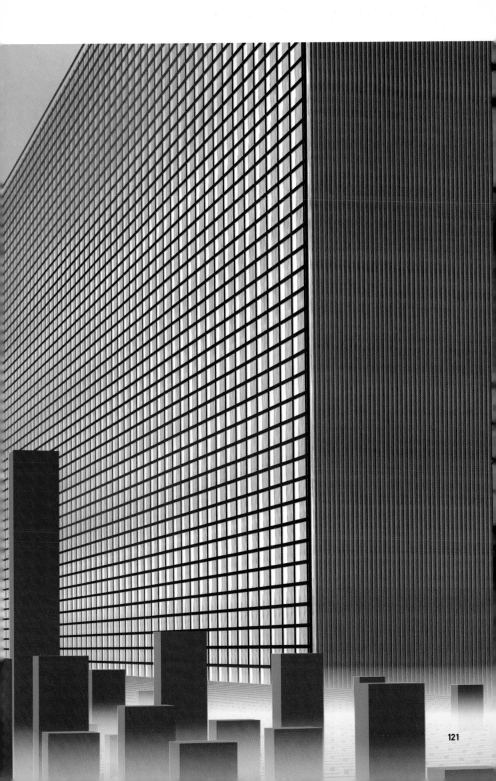

To make this forest more attractive – in both ecological and economical terms – a mixture of birch, oak, pine and beech of various ages is planted. One square kilometer of such forest absorbs 575 tons of CO_2 per year.

To absorb all CO_2, a mixed forest of 4,090,211 km^2 is needed – an enlargement of the former forest by 139%. This forest equals 26 times the surface of the total Datatown. When stacked on the area delegated for forests, 349 stories results. With 20-meter-high spaces and 5-meter-deep soil, the structure reaches a height of 8,725 meters.

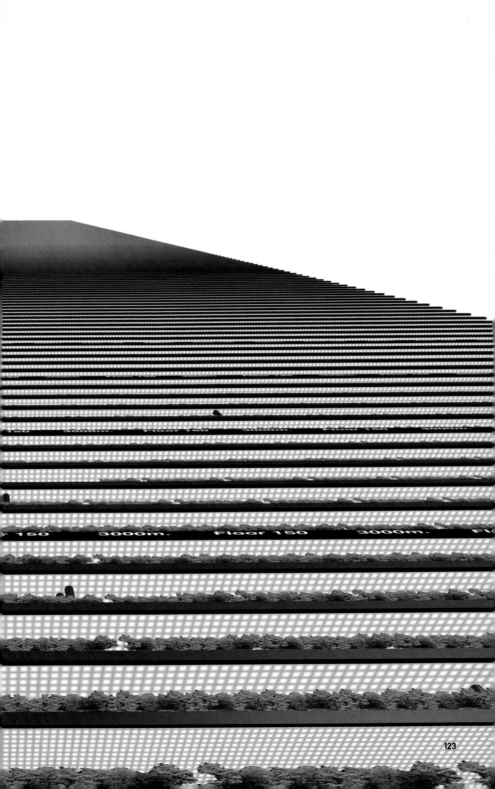

Floor 150   3000m.   Floor 150   3000m.

150   3000m.   Floor 150   3000m.   Fl

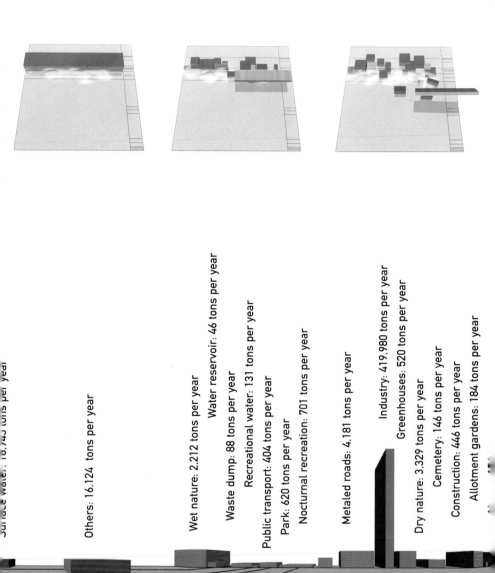

Surface water: 16.745 tons per year

Others: 16.124 tons per year

Wet nature: 2.212 tons per year

Water reservoir: 46 tons per year

Waste dump: 88 tons per year

Recreational water: 131 tons per year

Public transport: 404 tons per year

Park: 620 tons per year

Nocturnal recreation: 701 tons per year

Metaled roads: 4.181 tons per year

Industry: 419.980 tons per year

Greenhouses: 520 tons per year

Dry nature: 3.329 tons per year

Cemetery: 146 tons per year

Construction: 446 tons per year

Allotment gardens: 184 tons per year

buildings will result:

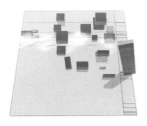

Agriculture: 88.241 tons per year

Living: 8.206 tons per year

output, it produces the highest tower.

3,834 stories that reaches a height of more than 100 km.

Sector Industry becomes a stacked Ruhr Valley.

3,800 m
152nd floor

3,800 m

3,800 m

3,800 m

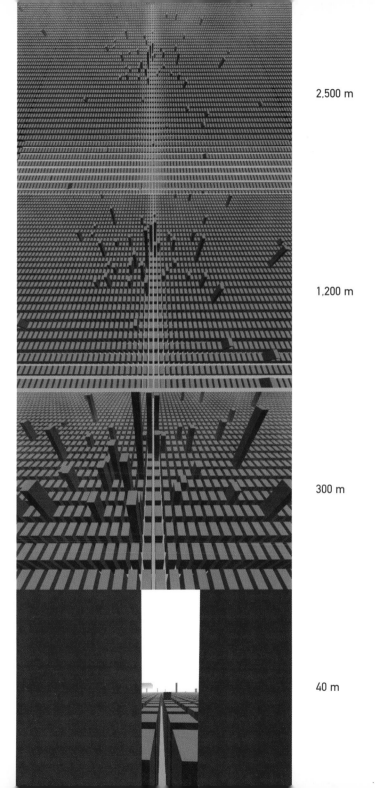

2,500 m

1,200 m

300 m

40 m

These forest-towers monumentalize economy and ecology.

If we produced all energy with windmills, the total CO_2 output will be reduced by 29.7%. 1 km^2 of windmills replaces 37.7 km^2 of CO_2 machines. This lowers the total forest by 75 floors. The industry tower is reduced by 45% or 1,725 floors.

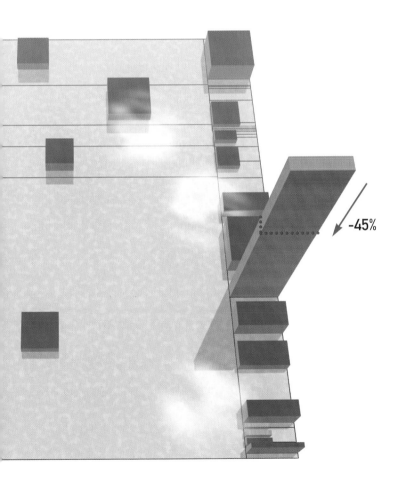

-45%

You are entering Sector Energy.
The reserved area equals 4,000 km^2.

Let us assume that all energy, in Datatown,
is produced by windmills. The most efficient
windmill produces 1 MW of power per year; since
a maximum of 10.1 of these windmills can be
placed in 1 km^3, the most efficient windmill park
produces 10.1 MW per km^2. Datatown needs
77,860 MW of electricity per year; this means a
windmill park totalling 77,860 km2. This is half
of Datatown. If this is concentrated in the reserved
area, a fringe-zone of 10 by 400 km, it would give
Datatown a 'turbo-facade' of 760 m in height: 19
layers of windmills.

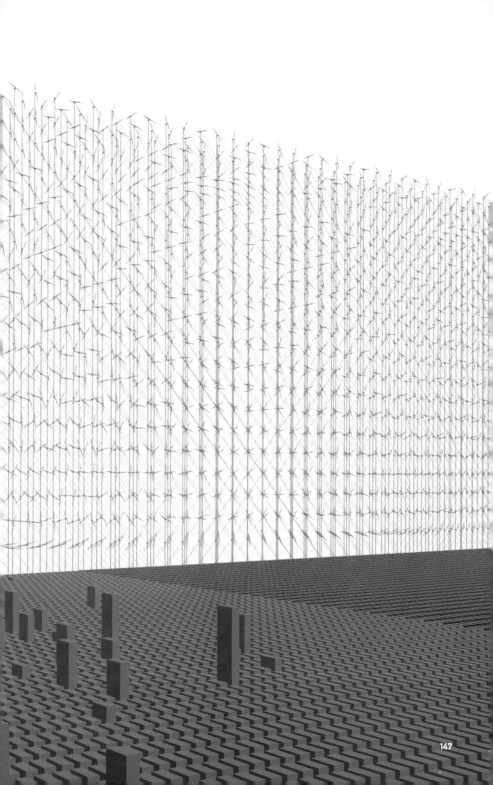

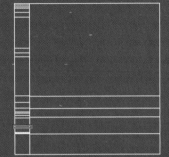

You are entering Sector Waste.
The reserved area for this sector is 328 km^2.

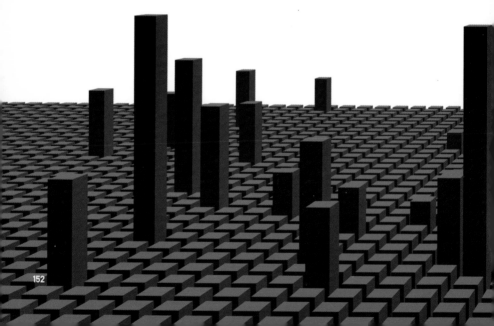

1,525,906 m^3 hill with a height of 73 meters.

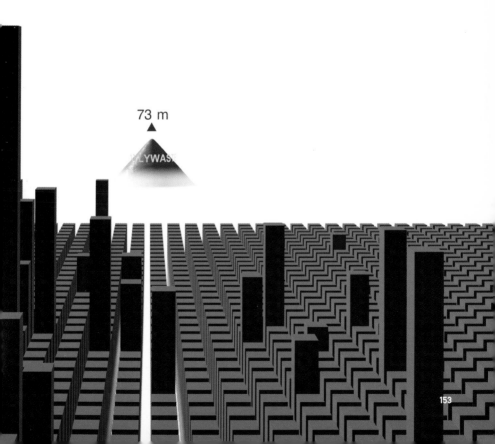

73 m

▲

In one month, this hill will increase to 9,475,917 tons,

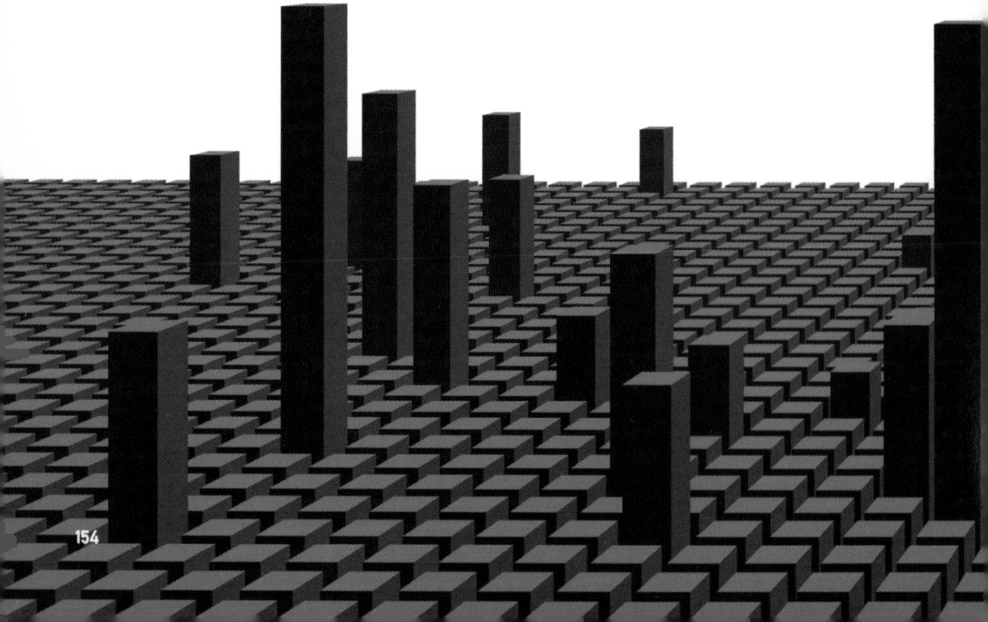

or 45,777,181 m^3.

229 m

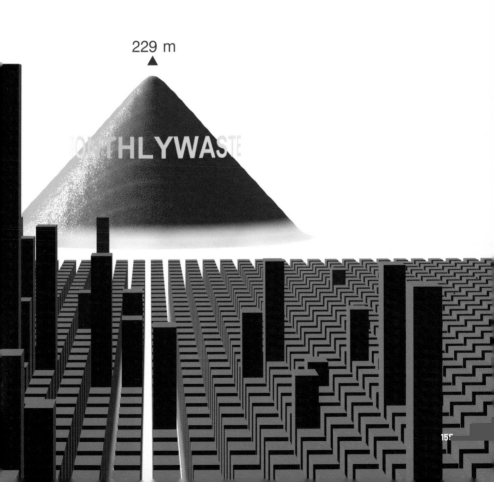

In one year, Datatown produces 1,137,711,000 tons of waste,

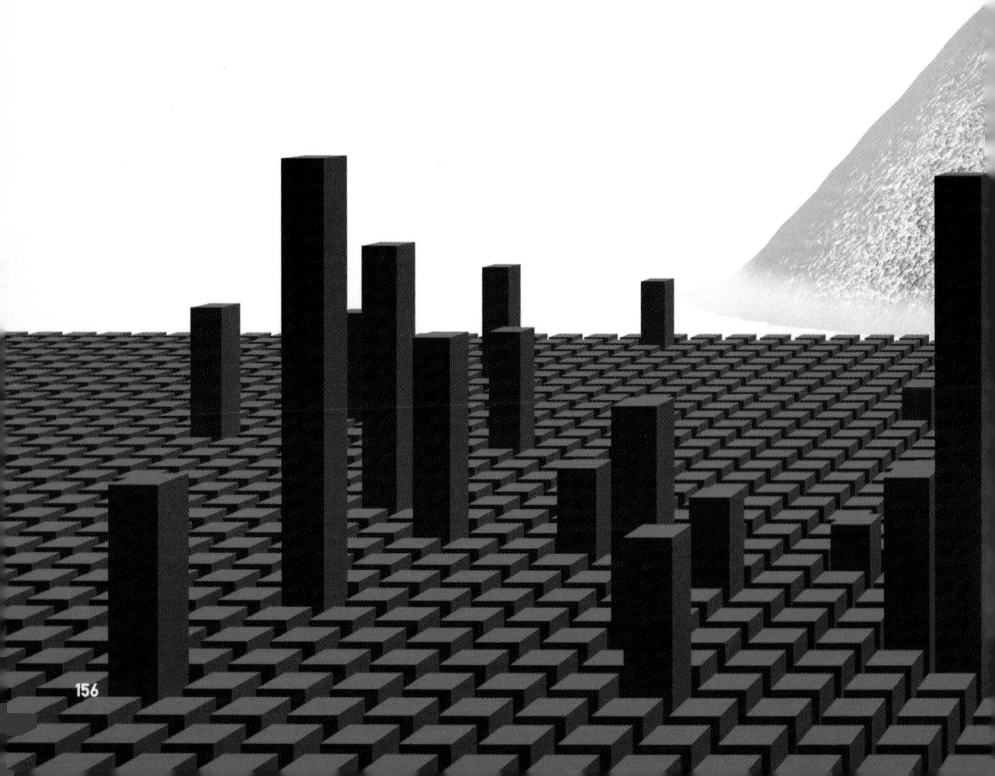

or a hill of 549,326,184 m³.

524 m
▲

EARLYWASTE

If one selects and sorts the waste, subdividing it into different

piles, a mining landscape of hills emerges.

One year of waste production...

Dredging sludge
560,300,000 tons

Bulky household
11,320,000 tons

Office, shop, and service
35,270,000 tons

Construction and demolition
25,410,000 tons

Hazardous
16,620,000 tons

Used tires
662,000 tons

Vehicle wrecks
1,555,000 tons

Blasting grit
678,000 tons

Agricultural refuse
14,780,000 tons

Household
52,745,000 tons

Process
62,630,000 tons

Sewage
37,440,000 tons

Litter, street cleaning
14,650,000 tons

Used oil
200,000 tons

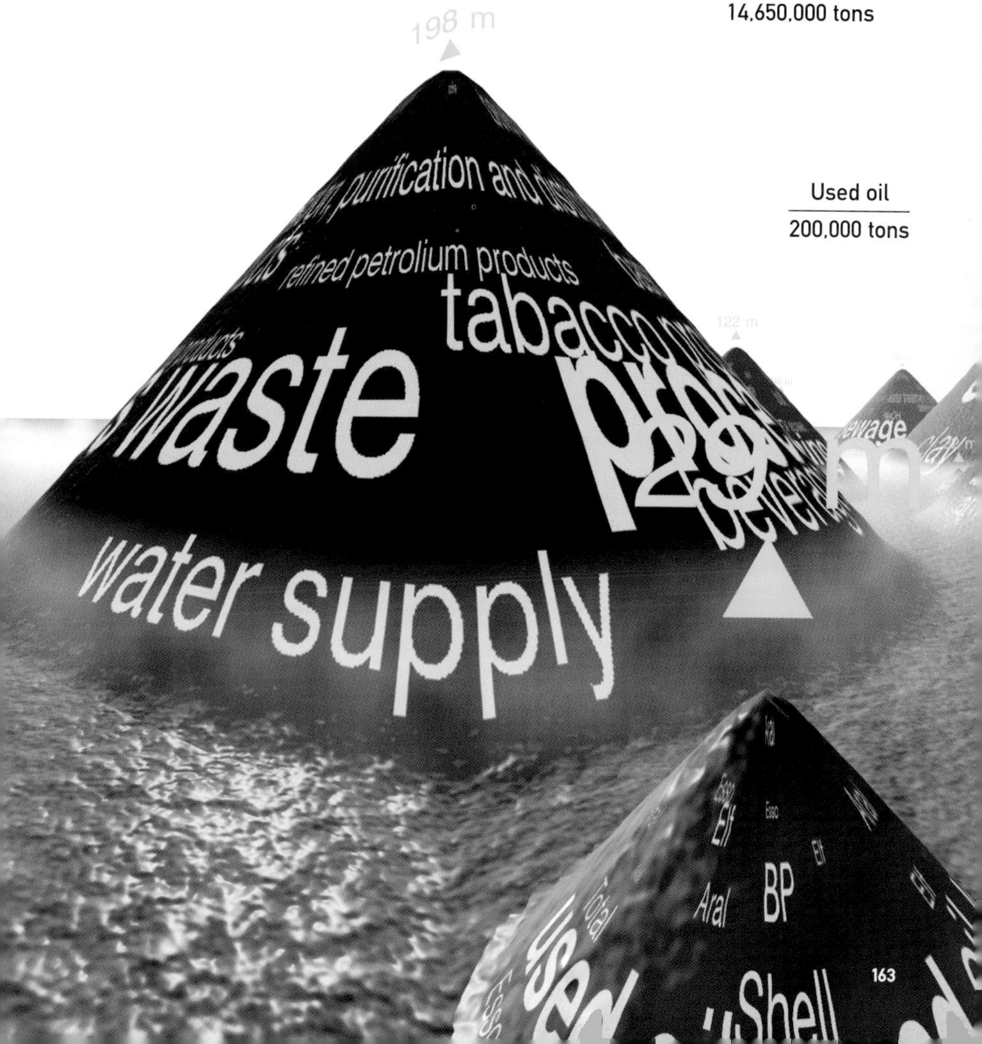

198 m

122 m

purification and

refined petrolium products

tabacco

waste

water supply

beverage

Esso
Elf
Aral
BP
Shell

163

Total available area for waste: 327 km^2.

After 150 years this area is filled.

Waste cannot spread any further.

It will have to grow vertically.

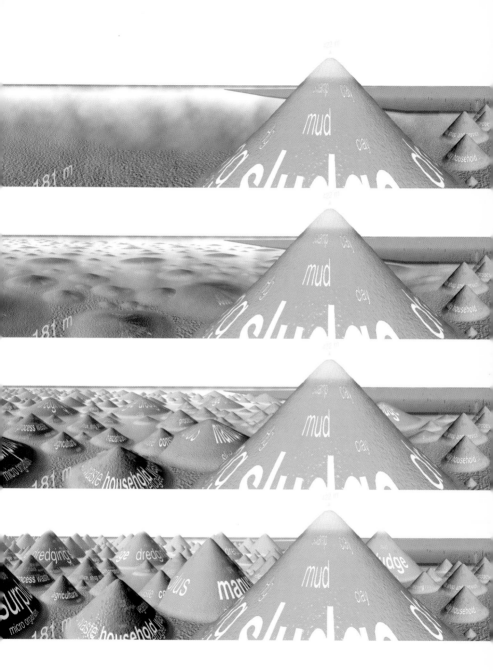

165

Yearly waste production

Household waste	52,745,000 tons
Bulky household waste	11,319,000 tons
Litter, street-cleaning waste, public garden	14,645,400 tons
Office, shop and service waste	35,266,000 tons
Process waste (non-hazardous)	62,631,800 tons
Hazardous waste	16,524,200 tons
Combustion residues from coal fired Chemical plants	0 tons
Construction and demolition waste	25,410,000 tons
Agricultural refuse	14,784,000 tons
Specific hospital waste	92,400 tons
Vehicle wrecks	1,555,400 tons
Used tires	662,200 tons
Ship-cleaning residues	11,565,400 tons
Used oil	200,200 tons
Blasting grit	677,600 tons
Contaminated soil	7,084,000 tons
Dredging sludge	560,282,800 tons
Phosphogypsum	22,422,400 tons
Sewage and waste-water-treatment sludge	37,437,400 tons
Manure surplus	261,800,000 tons
Total	1,137,105,200 tons

Yearly waste production (no recycling)

Household waste	95,079,600 tons
Bulky household waste	17,802,400 tons
Litter, street-cleaning waste, public garden	14,645,400 tons
Office, shop and service waste	46,970,000 tons
Process waste (non-hazardous)	108,831,800 tons
Hazardous waste	17,402,000 tons
Combustion residues from coal fired Chemical plants	18,480,000 tons
Construction and demolition waste	214,830,000 tons
Agricultural refuse	34,034,000 tons
Specific hospital waste	92,400 tons
Vehicle wrecks	6,237,000 tons
Used tires	1,247,400 tons
Ship-cleaning residues	11,565,400 tons
Used oil	1,078,000 tons
Blasting grit	1,001,000 tons
Contaminated soil	7,330,400 tons
Dredging sludge	560,282,800 tons
Phosphogypsum	22,422,400 tons
Sewage and waste-water-treatment sludge	50,419,600 tons
Manure surplus	261,800,000 tons
Total	1,491,551,600 tons

610 m
▲

years it will become a dolomitic landscape.

plaster

beam

dem

window frame

HEA 500

glass

concrete

plaster

beam

dem

window frame

HEA 500

glass

concrete

plaster

beam

dem

window frame

HEA 500

concrete

beam

heavy metals

bike, street, bu

can

plastic,

phosphogypsum

phosphogypsum

gypsum

IPE 360

column

reinforced con

rockwool

reinforced con

ition

W

beam

column

household

cardboard

iron

household waste household

cardboard

string glass, iron

IPE 360

column

colum

rockwool

reinforced con

reinforced con

paper

ition

column

glass

iron

beam

cardboard

textile

glass

paper

rope

glass

iron

ardboard

al refuse

tomatoes

kidney beans

tomatoes

bananas rice flax

IPE 360

rockwool

kidne

agricultu

beam

peas

corn

 a

(NHOOCH)

CH CH (NHOOCH)

vehicle

beans

If each sector stores its waste within its own boundaries, some mountains of their own waste.

Waste range

sectors will remain quite flat, while others will become

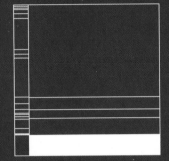

You are entering Sector Water.
The reserved area for this sector is 18,990 km^2.
46.2 km^2 is dedicated to the production and storage of drinking water, 18,943.8 km^2 to non-treated water.
Each year Datatown consumes 227,000,000,000,000 liters or 227.92 km^3 of water.

(C)O$_2$ forest	4.52 km^3
Agriculture	33.97 km^3
Greenhouses	0,20 km^3
Alotment gardens	0.07 km^3
Nature	1.28 km^3
Industry	177.1 km^3
Living area	10.78 km^3

Of all water consumption only 10.2% needs to be of 'spa quality'. This means that 23.1 km^3 of drinking water reservoirs and 204.82 km^3 of non-treated water basins have to be installed.

All non-treated water is stored in the surface water sector

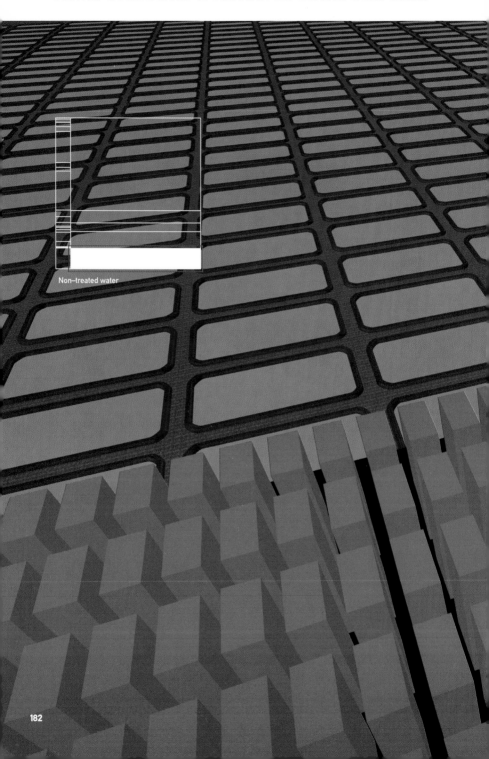

Non–treated water

(18,954 km^2). It leads to a series of basins with a depth of 10.8 m.

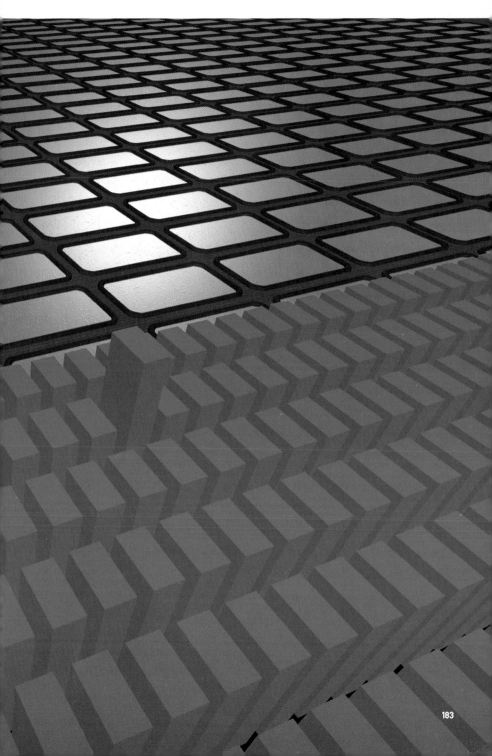

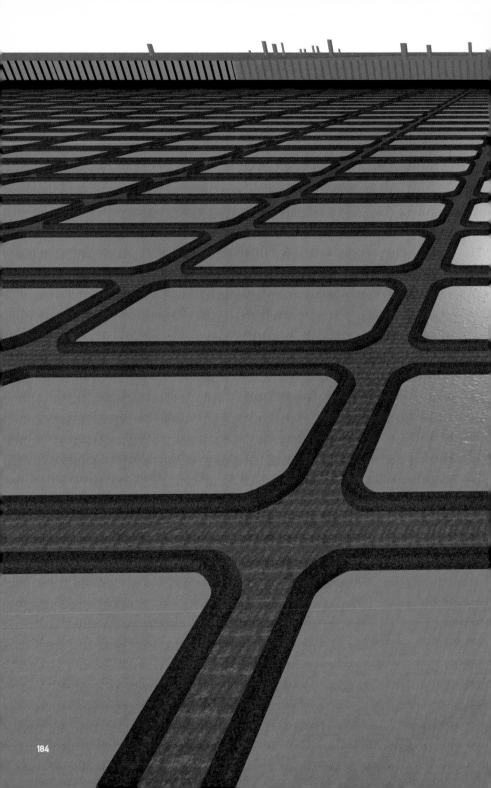

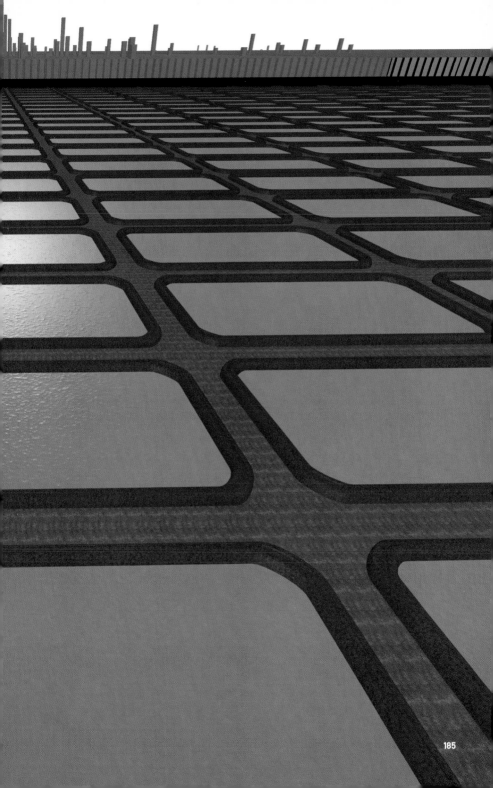

The 23.1 km³ of drinking water is stored in the 'water-storage-

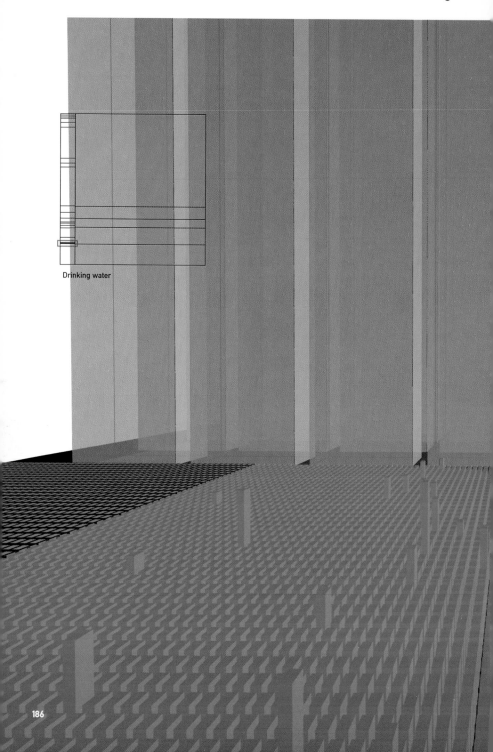

Drinking water

sector' (46.2 km^2).

It demands a 500-meter-high water 'column'.

If all required water is stored as snow, the total (227 x 6 =)
as a 4.2-meter 'blanket'.

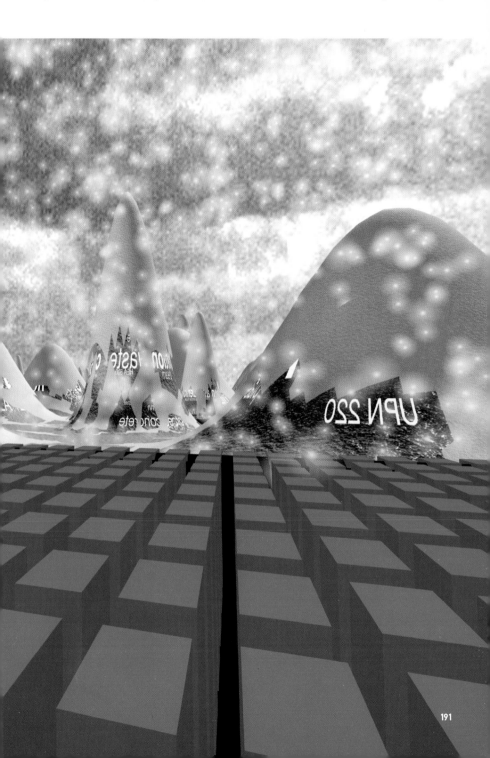

Snow in Sector Waste

Based on the statistics of the Alpine resort Chamonix, these 'mountains' can accommodate 1,167,857 visitors. With a year-round season, 206 shifts of 1.7 days each are needed for every inhabitant of Datatown to ski once a year. In 1998 6% of the (Dutch) population went skiing. Each of these 14,464,440 inhabitants of Datatown can ski 12.38 days per year.

Chamonix:
Available beds:	20,000
Lenght of slopes:	140 km
Average width of slope:	40 m
Total piste area:	5.6 km^2
Piste area per visitor:	280 m^2

Source: Syndicat d'Initiative Chamonix (France)

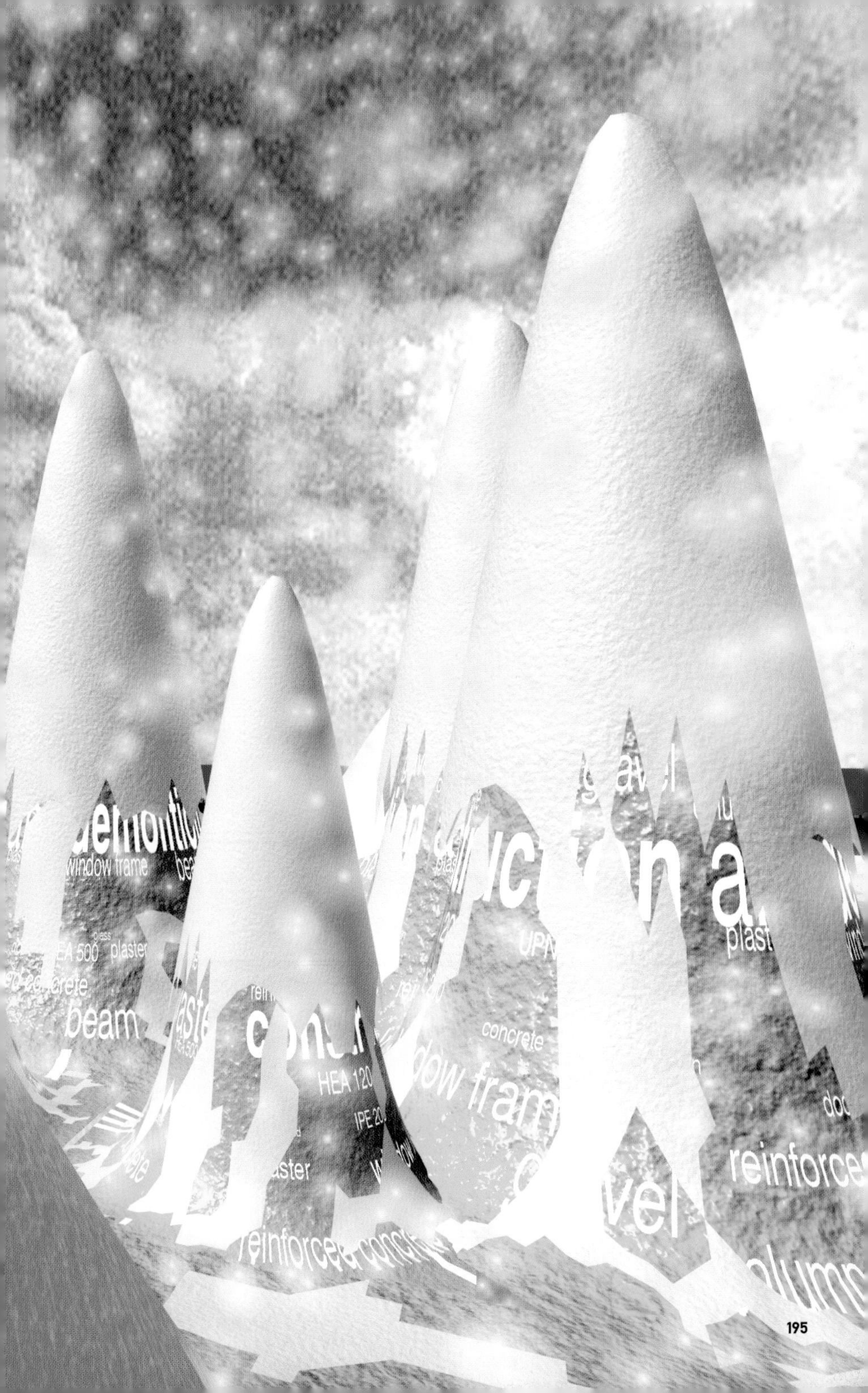
window frame
HEA 500
plaster
beam
concrete
HEA 120

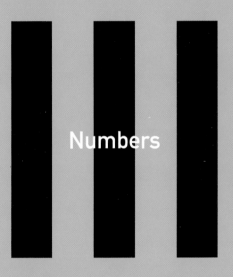

Numbers

WM   JvG

Numbers

Interviews with Arno van der Mark, Jan van Grunsven, A. W. H. Docters van Leeuwen, Hans van der Cammen, and Ronald van Tienhoven by Winy Maas, at Stroom, Center for the Visual Arts, The Hague, February 1999.

WM: Globalization and 'scaling up' are no longer empty terms. Municipalities in the Netherlands have become the Netherlands; the Netherlands has become the Benelux; the Benelux has become Europe; Europe is now the G7. And Al Gore's recent attempts to discontinue agricultural subsidies to Europe can be related to the fact that nowadays regional and urban planning are more than just local matters. Architecture and art went 'global' quite a while back. One of the ways in which this grand scale manifests itself is in the realm of numbers – in the world of statistics, which records changes, trends, and developments, and on the basis of which we claim to have a grasp of reality and to be able to assess the future. But despite the illusion of reality and truth, numbers don't exist without intuition. A number free of influence, free of interpretation, is inconceivable. A good example is the recent charge aimed at the agency that measures environmental and noise pollution at Amsterdam's Schiphol Airport. The agency was accused of relying too heavily on computer models and of not getting enough of its data in the field. This meant, allegedly, that its contribution to the annual environmental balance now required by the Ministry of Environmental Protection was its own invention – a made-up space. This fictitious or non-fictitious world of numbers is what I'd like to talk about. About the

AvdM

JvG

truth or untruth involved, about the sense and nonsense, and about the power and powerlessness. Through a series of discussions this evening, I'd like to get more information on, and insight into, the various spheres in which we find 'the number' and 'numbers'.

Numbers and Art

In 1998 in The Hague, artists Arno van der Mark and Jan van Grunsven intervened in a public area, the Schenkstrook, where they created a 24-hour street by installing daylight lamps. Dominated by its public nature, the space lacked any element of mystery. To mark the occasion, the artists also presented 'Limited Quotes', part of an event called 'Metacity', which also included MVRDV's 'Datatown'. In this video presentation, they give a vision of urbanism as it is currently presented in the media.

WM: What do you think is the nature of contemporary public space?
JvG: Public space in the classical sense – a representational model of 'the communal' – no longer exists. It has been replaced by the space of 'transition'. If we look at today's society, we see a high degree of individualism. But I think that as long as the individual has a need for a space to 'meet' or a space to share a common interest, we have to consider the meaning and form of those spaces. The current tendency to occupy the public space by individuals and institutions will only grow. We're entering an era with a broad range of individual activities and

initiatives, each of which attempts to lend shape to that which you may call public space, but which hasn't been designed as such. AvdM: At the moment, we have a new kind of public space. It's a communicational space, like the Internet. Public space has been altered into a kind of 'traffic', a coming and going. I think a new relationship will emerge between that which is interior and that which is exterior. The result will be an obvious decomposition of what has been known up until now as public space. WM: At the moment that you're saying this, is the role that art plays in public space different? JvG: Maybe the role of the artist is less elevated than it was 50 or 100 years ago, but that doesn't make it less important. If we're talking about the significance of each discipline that considers itself responsible for the design of the public domain, there is, in any case, a general shift occurring. The artist enters a situation that can be compared to that of the architect, whose work is always accompanied by conditions, and in this sense the architect contributes to the design of public space – a space with a multifunctional character. AvdM: Unlike the architect, the artist has no program. He can inflate existing programs in a more or less selfless way and operate within them on a very specific level. In so doing, he can expose areas that don't currently exist in the visual arts. As far as that's concerned, it's a very young profession. WM: I noticed your use of the word 'inflate', which is, in essence, taking one or more aspects to extremes – pushing a hypothesis, a reality, or a premise to its outer limits. This relates to techniques that have become generally accepted in physics and statistics: the extrapolation of various matters. Is this something that you deliberately choose to do in your art, in your interventions into public space? JvG: Yes. I'll give you an example of an older project. Someone wanted a work of art in an urban center. I found the design rather dubious and classical. My question was: are residents interested in what we call public space at the moment that it becomes their personal property? I suggested that part of the center be purchased from the municipality to be privatized by all inhabitants. The project made suggestions for the finance and mapped the juridical implications. The design was never realized, since it failed to make it past the first level – the Art Committee. WM: The act of 'taking things to extremes' seems to attach itself solidly to 'data' and to want to influence existing data. This zeroes in on the recent trend to gather and manipulate data as a means of penetrating and influencing the complexity of the world, of public space. What we have here is a culture of the number. This has repercussions for you as well. AvdM: Numbers play a role if you want to analyze situations or if you want to be aware of 'risk'. We're in a risk-filled society, and gradually the design – in terms of form and material – will disappear. The number will be important in allowing the discipline to formulate the critical standpoint needed to force a breakthrough in dealing with a co-party or client. This is an aspect that can alter a design practice. Personally, I use the number to reach a hypothesis when I'm working on a commission or taking a certain position. WM: It seems as though you're translating the word 'number' as 'argument'. That you see more of a culture of the argument than a culture of the number in what I've said. JvG: But that's evident, isn't it? Statistics are often used as proof in an argument. Statistics can substantiate arguments. They can also add a dialectical element to matters that are much more complex in reality. WM: Does that mean that in your minds artistry and intuition are shifting to some degree, and that the alienating aspect that art had back in the seventies is less relevant in this work? AvdM: Art has always been a representational discipline, and this aspect is simply disappearing. Art will have to demand a new role within practices still to be formulated. It will have to look for a practice and establish a new discipline. I also think that art has to make an effort to find different partners. Art has to evolve into new areas that will offer it a new role. This is part of your practice, and nobody else can do this for you. You have to develop the opportunities yourself.

Numbers and Administration

Jurist A. W. H. Docters van Leeuwen has been, among other things, head of the Dutch Secret Service and chairman of the Board of Procurator Generals, which served the Public Prosecutor. He is currently chairman of the Stichting Toezicht Effectenverkeer, a foundation that monitors market activity. On the occasion of the seventh Johan de Witt Lecture – held on 5 November 1998, in the Grote Kerk in Dordrecht – Docters van Leeuwen spoke on the organization of the Netherlands.

WM: Some time ago, while reading the magazine *Vrij Nederland*, I was struck by your vision of the Netherlands. In a short article on the Johan de Witt Lecture, you analyzed the way in which the Netherlands is slowly evaporating. The interesting aspect for architects and artists is perhaps the second part of your lecture, in which you suggest a different way of seeing the Netherlands. Can you explain this vision in more detail? DvL: In that lecture, I stated that the Netherlands is evaporating mentally, that a number of values that we have always experienced as being typically Dutch are losing their power of expression. And that because of this and because of the advance of pluralism, the Nether-lands is evaporating physically as well. Typical Dutch characteristics, such as the landscapes and the clear distinction between urbanism and rurality, are disappearing. We used to look down on the Belgians and their uncontrolled ribbon development. We were so proud that we didn't have that here. And now if you look at certain areas you see that

WM & DvL

ribbon-like rows of buildings are indeed lining the highways.
One type of ribbon development lines the highway from Amsterdam
to Rotterdam. Hardly any free space remains along that road. It bothers
me that this dis-orderly process is even being applauded. In *Steden
zonder horizon* (Cities With No Horizon), someone mentions 'carpet
cities': an intricate tapestry that we're supposed to think is attractive.
In my opinion it's not at all attractive. I like the look of a compact city.
We're starting to look like Los Angeles here, and everybody is completely fed up with it. If you want to preserve the Netherlands, the first thing
you have to do is accept urbanization, and then you have to design the
country as a megacity. That's the heart of my message. You have to dare
to stop thinking in terms of a country and to start thinking in terms of
a city. You have to dare to design the whole as one spatial concept.

*The city that I envision is a well-ordered city, with recognizable areas in
which not everything is prohibited per se, but in which various features
take center stage – landscape in one area, untouched nature in another,
cultivated nature here, housing and employment there; and clear-cut
areas somewhere else would give top priority to industry, aviation,
agriculture, or water. This would spark my enthusiasm: a free city
oriented toward trade, intelligence, industry, and nature, with a power-
ful, well-ordered dynamic. If Hong Kong and Singapore can do it under
much more difficult circumstances, why can't we?*
– A. W. H. Docters van Leeuwen, from 'The Johan de Witt Lecture,'
Vrij Nederland, 17 November 1998.

WM: You blame this evaporation largely on the administrative situation in the Netherlands. What do you think is the problem with the present administrative situation in this country? Can you conceive of a better form of government for the Netherlands, which you envision as a city with a population of about 15 million? DvL: I've done some figuring on the subject. You now have 14 departments, 12 provinces, and about 600 municipalities, all of which are authorized to make decisions in the area of physical planning. If you multiply 600 by 12 by 14, you get 98,800. All of them are involved in industrial and economic business-establishment policies. It shouldn't surprise you then to see a sanitary-napkin factory going up in the middle of a field of bent grass. The line of thought aimed at creating a new form of administration has been around for awhile. I once proposed establishing a single national level and 44 regions. That's it. Nothing else. The point is that you end up with a much clearer, much simpler administrative structure, in which one half of the administration has jurisdiction over matters that the other does not have. I'd gladly allow the national level to make major physical-planning decisions, but I'd want to see democratic supervision as part of the package. These are the kind of models I have in mind. The 44 regions could be concentrated around centrally located municipalities and main traffic arteries. You'd keep looking for areas of urban concentration and places at which transportation axes are located. Based on these data, you would then divide the Netherlands into 44 regions as has also suggested by Elko Brinkman. Later, it was simplified to 22 regions. I now think that's a better idea, because the plan needs a somewhat larger scale. WM: That means that the critical size for an ideal administration shifted in a relatively short time. How does that strike you? We have to be self-critical when it comes to changes on an international level too. Does your model allow for this? DvL: You have to be administratively fluid; you have to make continual adjustments. The army does it, for example. If it's absolutely necessary, then it happens, but apparently it's not considered necessary at the administrative level, or those involved just don't feel any urgency when it comes to change. WM: Sometimes it's said that disaster scenarios are needed to bring about this sort of change. Is this conceivable at the administrative level? DvL: I don't think so. You have two kinds of crises. You have acute crises, but also what we Dutch call 'the frog in the pan.' If you put a frog in a pan filled with cold water and slowly warm the water over a fire, he won't jump out. He'll just stay there, nice and content, and end up as boiled frog. I think it's this second kind of crisis that we're dealing with. People don't see what's happening; nor do they see that they – even in a highly pluralistic society – are always able to determine their fate to some degree or another. There's always something that can be influenced, if not created. To stick with art – we say that artists best able to express the times in which they live are the greatest artists. Apparently there's an interplay between the act of influencing culture and that culture itself. You can influence it, even though you can't create it, can't force it into a mold of your own making. This may have been possible at one time, but not any more. An administrator cannot hope to create society – I don't think that's possible – but he can use his influence to promote a certain degree of harmony. WM: The model that you proposed earlier in this discussion was about forming regions selected on the basis of characteristics – a concept that *does* evoke the idea of a certain capacity to create. DvL: Yes, but it's not easy to start out by saying what can be created and what's going to depend on future developments. For example, we've all become much freer thanks to the personal computer, but each of us has Microsoft architecture built into that computer. We're talking about huge, organizational decisions. Even in this day and age, there are obviously very large organizational principles to be considered. These are so big that we aren't even aware of them, but they do exist. For that matter, something strange is occurring in the area of rules and regulations. Everyone wants rules. You never hear anyone saying that he wants fewer regulations. But what happens is that these rules are not implemented. Fewer and fewer regulations are being enforced. The symbolic value and the benefit seem to be in the *demand* for regulations and in the *issuing* of regulations, not in their enforcement. WM: If we go back to your observation that regions are based on geographical differences, then you should be able to make the formation of regions even easier by increasing those differences. You could say, for instance: let's not have a port in Amsterdam; let's concentrate all port activities in Rotterdam and give the whole tourist package to Amsterdam, and so on. Can you imagine the Netherlands within the framework of this creation of regions as a series of 'Grand Projects', each of which has a very specific nature – one vast airport, for example, one forested expanse, one great river, one high mountain, one big city? DvL: It wouldn't work that way exactly, of course. You have to leave room for the unexpected as well. But, yes, to a very limited extent. It is un-Dutch, but that doesn't mean it's wrong. It's happening elsewhere, with success. Dutch ideas on intimate urbanism are not compatible with the concept of the Grand Project. WM: In creating regions, 'interdependency' – currently a very popular term in the philosophy of culture – is an important factor in the coherence of the whole. In other words, the more specialized mutual parties in one region or another become, the more they're going to rely on one another. What one lacks, the other has, and vice versa. Some people find it an interesting European model. I can imagine that the same model could also be used to create regions in the Netherlands. DvL: Taking the acceptance of urbanism as a point of departure, I think that there's no other way to go. It's a continuation of the discussion on Grand Projects. Only I'd be happier seeing them 'come into being.' Otherwise I see an excess of Napoleonic features, and I'm not sure that we're ready for that. WM: 'Coming into being' and 'influencing' are almost neighbors. You could promote the history of development – use the media to get your message across. As far as that's concerned, I think that your administrative ideas would have a chance to find a place within public opinion. DvL: I don't see much of it in official politics. Apparently there's something that keeps this sort of thinking from penetrating. Speaker in the audience: If everyone would just take personal responsibility, wouldn't the problem be solved?

What would it be like to live in a megacity, with the Asian dynamic whizzing in your ears, but also with areas of real scenic beauty offering peace and quiet? Wouldn't it be sensible to develop a framework in which pluralism can evolve as a positive force?
– A. W. H. Docters van Leeuwen, from 'The Johan de Witt Lecture,' *Vrij Nederland,* 17 November 1998.

DvL: I think that would only make it worse. What we're dealing with are pluralistic developments characterized by a high degree of individualism, by varying lifestyles, by strongly differing perceptions of reality, and of the metaphysical. This kind of pluralism takes unbearable forms. You can handle this in two ways. The first is by saying: ' go with the flow', which makes this pluralism more bearable – you move in the direction that you seem to be headed for anyway. You can also say: no, I must and shall find harmony. I must and shall find the common denominator, the common interest. And, still keeping your question in mind, this is something that *everyone* has to do, because otherwise it won't work. My conclusion is that it won't succeed if perceptions of reality differ. This is one of the problems we're facing – you can no longer say that one perception of rationality is better than another. This has major consequences, because the fact is that we define reality through rationality. But if you can no longer say that one version of rationality transcends another, something strange happens – you don't have to listen to one another anymore. This means that finding the common interest becomes a completely different kind of task, and that it may be easier to find it in your well-perceived individuality than in a diligent search for the responsibility that is yours as part of the public interest.

Numbers and Physical Planning

Hans van der Cammen, physical planner, formerly worked for the research organization TNO. He recently joined the Government Physical Planning Agency and is now helping to develop the Fifth Report on Physical Planning. Not long ago the preliminary study for this report, nicknamed the 'Charcoal Sketch,' was presented.

WM: In the amazingly short period of only six months, your agency has created a new sketch of the perspective for the Netherlands over a period of the next 20 years. One of the techniques used in recent years in making structure plans is to quickly set up a large team that then produces more than 20 models. What was your approach to this national structural concept, and how many people are now working on this project? HvdC: One of the tasks inherited by the new cabinet created in 1998 was to draw up, in six months time, a preliminary report on the organization of the Netherlands. At the Ministry for Housing, Physical Planning, and Environment (VROM), which was ultimately given the job, a small group of four or five people went to work. People from other departments, who were asked to comment on the proceedings, numbered about 20. It all went so fast because much discussion and research had already taken place, some of which was organized by the ministers, but often also by others. All the information made available to us in this manner became a breeding ground, which allowed us to start working almost immediately. WM: You're educated as a physical planner. Does that mean that you grew up with statistics?

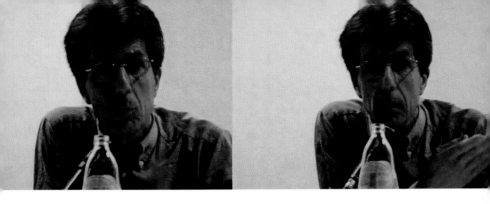

HvdC: Although they are bound, the number and physical planning have a rocky marriage. In the end, you have very little chance of collecting all the data related to numbers and using it to make good plans. In some cases, only behavior that relates closely to technique, such as traffic patterns, or perhaps birth rates, can be useful in helping you to compile hard numbers. But physical planning usually has to rely on spatial models and on estimates to reach a certain prognostic calculation. It's more like pure guesswork. The relationship between statistics and physical planning is not as close as you might think. WM: I can imagine that a kind of selection process takes place in planning. Certain decisions are extremely suited to the use of numbers – they elevate numbers to a polemic figure to rouse political decisiveness – while in other cases this isn't necessary. Are big decisions the ones more often based on numbers? HvdC: What you're asking touches on the project that gave rise to this gathering. In the Datatown Project you see an intensive use of numbers applied to physical planning: in shock scenarios or doom scenarios. These are images of the future that indicate a place at which you will be confronted with an inflexible barrier. Such a barrier can be illustrated quite well by using numbers. It's a very useful way to apply the number to physical planning. WM: How are shock scenarios like these implemented in practice? You risk falling into a kind of mediocrity if you don't use extreme scenarios in a very clear and precise manner. HvdC: I'll give you two examples. Docters van Leeuwen recommends a simpler administrative structure, but you could also consider going in the opposite direction.

You might think about how decisions could be reached not by limiting yourself to fewer deciders but, on the contrary – with the use of all available information science and networks – by giving the job to many more deciders. A number of experiments carried out in recent years make me optimistic. Maybe the government should invest more money in that area. It would be a great field of activity for physical planning. Another example in which shock scenarios play a role is that of the rising sea level. One of the leitmotifs in the preliminary report is the role that water will play during the next 100 years. A map in the report indicates everything that will disappear under water if the sea level rises by one meter in the future. If no measures are taken, most of the Netherlands will vanish below the surface of the water. Are you going to continue raising the level of the dikes, or are you going to approach the problem in a more random manner, calling on the use of more skill and resilience, and allowing the rising water to have its own way now and again? WM: It's fairly easy to take technological aspects and come up with shock scenarios or numbers. But in planning, is it also conceivable on a social level? HvdC: I don't know. We're becoming a society tremendously oriented toward individualization, sometimes to an absurd degree: everybody has his own target group. Of course this is a nightmare for planners and sociologists, because then you have to devise a different behavioral model for everyone. It means we no longer fit together into one model. As planners, if we don't have a model anymore, it becomes much harder. We can't predict our behavior anymore, and we don't know what's going to happen tomorrow. This behavioral aggregate is necessary to a planner – otherwise you really have to plan the entire society! Despite all this, you can see that an enormous number of individual decisions made every day still escort the Netherlands home at night in good condition. So I feel sure that every day we, as individuals, are making the right decisions. Imagine having to plan something like that – there's a real nightmare! WM: You're now focusing on the role of the individual. I imagine that creating a plan for a country or city-state like the Netherlands requires a sociological vision. HvdC: I like to find inspiration in someone like Manuel Castells, who offers a theme that can contribute a lot to today's physical planning. Castells gives us an intelligent analysis of the tension between globalization and the resulting movement, on the one hand, and, on the other, the reaction that we engrave into our individuality for the sake of our identity. We do this in our public space, but every district also has its own identifying mark. In my opinion, this is an example of a social theory that plays a role in physical planning. WM: This dichotomy between globalization and localization can be taken to extremes – in terms of both public administration, as Docters van Leeuwen just proposed, and physical planning. Do you see possibilities of putting this into action even more strongly in the near future? HvdC: It's possible. But for a government, of course, that would be it. Most administrative decisions are made in the smaller local units. Thus the preliminary report contains a certain amount of reform. As a national government, we're making an attempt not to manage everything in generic concepts that speak to the country as a whole. In the final (Fifth) Report, we'll try to aim our statements at individual regions, and we will no longer express ourselves in the form of general regulations applicable to the entire nation. WM: The program for the Netherlands of the future can be lengthy and 'spectacular'. It can be part of an international agenda. How far can you take such mental models on a national scale, and can this be further institutionalized in a laboratory? HvdC: I agree that you need to implement large-scale programs. Let's just make a couple of big projects though. A very good environmental plan for the Netherlands would be one such project. The question is who should realize it. You have to cope with the administration's slow-moving nature, of course, but ultimately you manage. WM: Do you also see the Netherlands as a city? Do you think that a critical border has been crossed, that the amalgamation of cities and towns should now produce urban forms, and that these should be discussed as an entity? HvdC: In a certain sense, we're already doing that. In the preliminary report, the Netherlands is presented as an entity. On the other hand, I think that

WM & Rvt

we're a nation of cities – a nation of cities plus many networks.
A metropolis is going a bit too far. We're not a metropolis. WM: We
don't have to be. This is about compact thinking. And as far as that's
concerned, I see a nation of cities as a kind of intermediate period, as
an overture to a somewhat more agrarian or flatter metropolis. HvdC:
I don't think I agree. Let's keep it simple. You can define a metropolis
by the cost of land. Land there is a luxury item. In my opinion, the
Randstad and the Ruhr are not metropolises. But it also has something
to do with planning. It would take an enormous steering operation to
elevate the Netherlands to a metropolitan status. And we're not heading
in the direction of a stronger planning function, but toward a more
moderate one.

Rvt

Numbers and Culture

Visual artist Ronald van Tienhoven advises the Mondrian Foundation
on matters concerning art in public space. At the moment he's working
with the Dutch artist Maarten de Reus on an exhibition about
information design, a new branch of graphic media.

WM: Can you explain your interest in information design? RvT: The
information designer organizes a variety of data into structures that
coordinate complex systems and processes in a clear way. It's precisely
in times like ours that an increasing need exists to represent – with the
use of maps, genealogical documents, statistics, diagrams, plans, and
other sources of information – the complexity of that which our society
produces. A major focus of information design is the way in which the
viewer links his own insights with the contents of such 'data packages'.
Information design is, therefore, a consequence of an increase in the
amount of information available to the public. The emergence of information design represents an important step toward making the public
domain – in both a physical and mental sense more 'public'. Information
design can be seen as a navigation system which, at its best, offers
insight into the processes that have created our complex society. WM:
What does this signify for art, or for the artist? RvT: If artists want to
relate to public space and to the public debate, they can no longer rely
solely on the tool kit that they've been using since time immemorial.
This insight has led to a number of exhibitions – including
METACITY/DATATOWN – which feature the demand for 'publicness',

whether demonstrated by disaster scenarios or dream-like fantasies. Collecting data and coupling it to decisions (art-related or utilitarian) are activities requiring a study that should have a certain visual quality in and of itself. Information design is a new phenomenon that deals with this visual quality. An attempt is made to produce a representation of data *not* based on its collection or to render it as tastefully as possible while producing a matchless marriage of quantities of complex information. In this way we try to distill a crystal-clear image. The result is more than a graphic interface; it's also a social interface. The discipline wants to optimize the exchange of information in order to clarify a given situation or process. In that respect it can show the consequences that this has for decision-making and for the positions held by administrative authorities within our society. After all, they should use this information to maintain a structure that is as clear and open as possible. It seems as if the openness of information needs to be redefined, not only through political or technocratical means, but also culturally. Subsequently, art has a role in that process. WM: Is your objective transparency, or is it also about distorting reality? RvT: Distortion can be very interesting. For instance, you can use cartographic legends to create an 'information landscape' that is perhaps not completely true but does refer to a scenario for the future, simply because it deviates from the conventional view. WM: To escape dead-end references to chaos theories, those in architecture are broaching the domains of the number, the study, and logic. Would this be a sensible and relevant direction for art to take as well? RvT: I don't think you can ever have a representation of absolute numbers or of abstract notions of numbers. The number must always relate to a physical reality. In METACITY/DATATOWN, an attempt has been made to compile a wealth of statistical data, accompanied by a graphic or visual picture that is subsequently shown within a certain period of time in order to reflect the laws of cause and effect as clearly as possible. As far as our relationship to public space is concerned, art and architecture should be able to take this information and use it with skill and sensitivity.

Hans van der Cammen pointed out that it's not possible to come up with a structural concept on the basis of hard numbers supplied by the administration. Apparently another kind of study – a more subjective study – is needed. What we need is a hybrid of some sort, a study that's part numbers and part signals. WM: How can these signals be represented within a numerical space? I'd be thrilled if we could put our finger on that critical moment of transition between laissez-faire and collective dynamism – whether it's at an administrative level, a level pertaining to our natural landscape, a de facto level, or a decision-making level. WM: 'Deviation' and 'dilemma' are also motives for unraveling the flow of information and data or to test their critical content. Can you see that being reflected in numerical space? RvT: The laws of cause and effect are indeed at the heart of this discussion. The problem is that causality and processing the consequences of our association with the laws of cause and effect are based largely on the method applied to your own discipline. Every professional group has developed its own Pavlovian reflex in order to cope with reality. If you'll just step outside the method of preparation that applies to your own discipline, you can develop a flexibility in your relationship to data and learn to use data, intelligently and sensibly, in your project. I'm becoming increasingly aware of the need for collaboration on an interdisciplinary level.

Credits

Metacity/Datatown
Installation photography: Hans Werlemann, Rotterdam
Cover, pages 1–7, 220–224

Metacity
Research: MVRDV – Winy Maas, Jacob van Rijs and Nathalie de
Vries with Bas van Neijenhof, Fokke Moerel, Gabriela Bojalil and
Penelope Dean

Mexico City
Video stills
Images grabbed from video by MVRDV – Winy Maas, Jacob van
Rijs and Nathalie de Vries with Bas van Neijenhof and Jose
Castillo, 091298
Statistics: MVRDV – Bas van Neijenhof and Gabriela Bojalil

São Paulo
Video stills
Images grabbed from video by MVRDV – Winy Maas, Jacob van
Rijs and Nathalie de Vries with Bas van Neijenhof and Patricia
Cezario Silva, 061298
Statistics: MVRDV – Bas van Neijenhof and Gabriela Bojalil

The Netherlands
Statistics: MVRDV – Bas van Neijenhof

Datatown
Hypotheses
Research and production: MVRDV – Winy Maas, Jacob van Rijs
and Nathalie de Vries with Bas van Neijenhof, Eline Wieland and
Marino Gouwens

Sector Living
Research and production: MVRDV – Winy Maas, Jacob van Rijs
and Nathalie de Vries with Bas van Neijenhof, Christoph
Schindler and Mathurin Hardel

Sector Agriculture

Research and production: MVRDV – Winy Maas, Jacob van Rijs and Nathalie de Vries with Bas van Neijenhof, Eline Wieland and Marino Gouwens

Sector (C)O$_2$

Research and production: MVRDV – Winy Maas, Jacob van Rijs and Nathalie de Vries with Bas van Neijenhof and Margeritha Salmeron Espinosa and Ximo Peris Casado. Based on studies by Toshiki Omatsu for 'Datascapes 2', a project lead by Winy Maas and Jacob van Rijs at the Berlage Institute, Amsterdam, 1998

Sector Energy

Research and production: MVRDV – Winy Maas, Jacob van Rijs and Nathalie de Vries with Bas van Neijenhof and Mathurin Hardel

Sector Waste

Research and production: MVRDV – Winy Maas, Jacob van Rijs and Nathalie de Vries with Bas van Neijenhof and Mathurin Hardel

Sector Water

Research and production: MVRDV – Winy Maas, Jacob van Rijs, and Nathalie de Vries with Bas van Neijenhof, Fokke Moerel, Christoph Schindler, Eline Wieland, and Marino Gouwens

Numbers

Interviews with Arno van der Mark, Jan van Grunsven, Mr. A.W.H. Docters van Leeuwen, Hans van der Cammen and Ronald van Tienhoven by Winy Maas at Stroom, Centre for the Visual Arts,The Hague, February 1st, 1999
Postscript by Marc Neelen and Piet Vollaard
Translations into English by D'Laine Camp & Donna de Vries-Hermansader.
Video stills by Bas van Neijenhof and Stroom, Center for Visual Arts, The Hague

References

Mexico City
United Nations Center for Human Settlements (Habitat).
An Urbanizing World: Report on Human Settlements. 1996.
United Nations Center for Human Settlements (Habitat).
CitiBase for dos (version 1.4.05). 1997.
United Nations Population Division. World Urbanization Prospects,
the 1994 Revision. New York: United Nations, 1995.
The Times Atlas of the World (Ninth Comprehensive Edition).
London: Times Books with Bartholomew, 1994.

São Paulo
United Nations Center for Human Settlements (Habitat).
An Urbanizing World: Report on Human Settlements. 1996.
United Nations Center for Human Settlements (Habitat).
CitiBase for dos (version 1.4.05). 1997.
United Nations Population Division. World Urbanization Prospects,
the 1994 Revision. New York: United Nations, 1995.
The Times Atlas of the World (Ninth Comprehensive Edition).
London: Times Books with Bartholomew, 1994.

The Netherlands
United Nations Center for Human Settlements (Habitat).
An Urbanizing World: Report on Human Settlements. 1996.
United Nations Center for Human Settlements (Habitat).
CitiBase for dos (version 1.4.05). 1997.
CBS Statistics Netherlands. Statistical Yearbook 1998
of the Netherlands. Voorburg/Heerlen, 1998.
De grote bosatlas (51st edition). Groningen: Wolters-Noordhoff
Atlasproducties, 1995.
Koten, Dick van, ed. A Bird's Eye View. Baarn,
The Netherlands: Tirion.
Hofmeester, Bart. 's-Gravenhage breed gezien. Rotterdam:
Phoenix & Den Oudsten,1987.
Amsterdam, Herman van. Bloemen achter de duinen.
Sassenheim: Rebo Productions, 1987.

Metacities compared
United Nations Center for Human Settlements (Habitat).
An Urbanizing World: Report on Human Settlements. 1996.
United Nations Center for Human Settlements (Habitat). CitiBase
for dos (version 1.4.05). 1997.

The Times Atlas of the World (Ninth Comprehensive Edition).
London: Times Books with Bartholomew, 1994.

Sector Living
Volkshuisvesting in cijfers. Den Haag: Ministerie van
Volkshuisvesting, Ruimtelijke Ordening en Milieubeheer, 1998.
CBS Statistics Netherlands. Statistical Yearbook 1998 of the
Netherlands. Voorburg/Heerlen, 1998.

Sector Agriculture
Landbouw-Economisch Instituut (LEI-DLO). De betekenis
van de landbouw voor de Nedelandse economie. 1995.
Landbouw-Economisch Instituut (LEI-DLO). Land- en
tuinbouwcijfers. 1998.
CBS Statistics Netherlands. Statistical Yearbook 1998
of the Netherlands. Voorburg/Heerlen, 1998.

Sector (C)O2
CBS Statistics Netherlands. Statistical Yearbook 1998 of the
Netherlands. Voorburg/Heerlen, 1998.
De grote bosatlas (51st edition). Groningen: Wolters-Noordhoff
Atlasproducties, 1995.

Sector Energy
CBS Statistics Netherlands. Statistical Yearbook 1998
of the Netherlands. Voorburg/Heerlen, 1998.

Sector Waste
CBS Statistics Netherlands. Statistical Yearbook 1998
of the Netherlands. Voorburg/Heerlen, 1998.
De grote bosatlas (51st edition). Groningen: Wolters-Noordhoff
Atlasproducties, 1995.

Sector Water
CBS Statistics Netherlands. Statistical Yearbook 1998
of the Netherlands. Voorburg/Heerlen, 1998.
Van Hall Instituut Business Center. Individuele Behandeling van
Afvalwater. 1998.
Koerselman, dr. W. ; Senden, ir. W. J. M. K.; Super, ir. J. MER
locatiekeuze grootschalige oppervlaktewaterwinning. KIWA, 1997.

The poplar, the most efficient tree for absorbing CO₂ in a Dutch climate

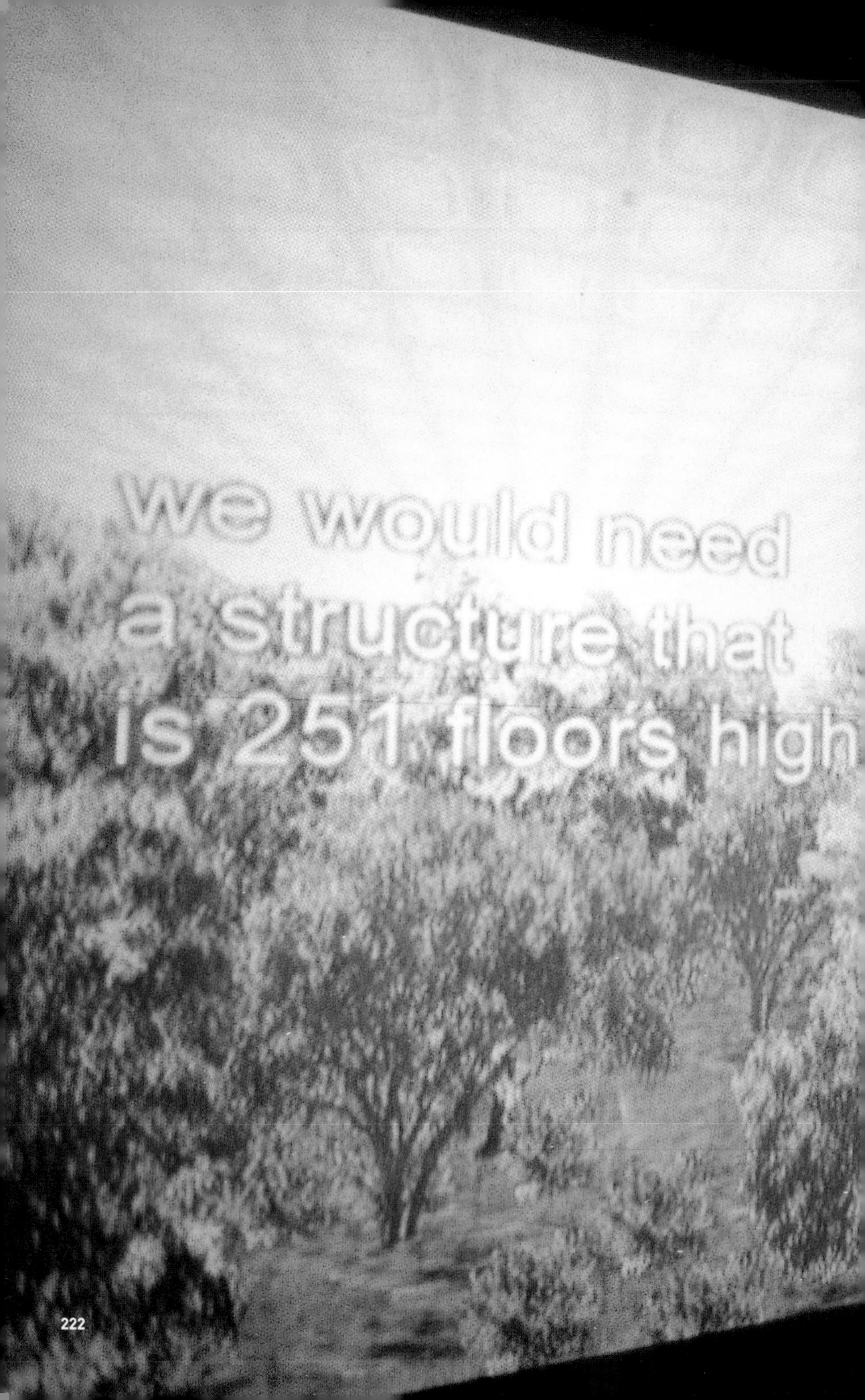

we would need
a structure that
is 251 floors high